T0323616

Cambridge Elements ≡

Elements in Current Archaeological Tools and Techniques
edited by
Hans Barnard
Cotsen Institute of Archaeology
Willeke Wendrich
Polytechnic University of Turin

WORKED BONE, ANTLER, IVORY, AND KERATINOUS MATERIALS

Adam DiBattista
American School of Classical Studies at Athens

COTSEN INSTITUTE OF
ARCHAEOLOGY AT UCLA

CAMBRIDGE
UNIVERSITY PRESS

Shaftesbury Road, Cambridge CB2 8EA, United Kingdom

One Liberty Plaza, 20th Floor, New York, NY 10006, USA

477 Williamstown Road, Port Melbourne, VIC 3207, Australia

314–321, 3rd Floor, Plot 3, Splendor Forum, Jasola District Centre,
New Delhi – 110025, India

103 Penang Road, #05–06/07, Visioncrest Commercial, Singapore 238467

Cambridge University Press is part of Cambridge University Press & Assessment,
a department of the University of Cambridge.

We share the University's mission to contribute to society through the pursuit of
education, learning and research at the highest international levels of excellence.

www.cambridge.org
Information on this title: www.cambridge.org/9781009532686

DOI: 10.1017/9781009181686

When citing this work, please include a reference to the DOI 10.1017/9781009181686

First published 2024

A catalogue record for this publication is available from the British Library

ISBN 978-1-009-53268-6 Hardback
ISBN 978-1-009-18167-9 Paperback
ISSN 2632-7031 (online)
ISSN 2632-7023 (print)

Additional resources for this publication at www.cambridge.org/DiBattista

Worked Bone, Antler, Ivory, and Keratinous Materials

Elements in Current Archaeological Tools and Techniques

DOI: 10.1017/9781009181686
First published online: December 2024

Adam DiBattista
American School of Classical Studies at Athens

Author for correspondence: Adam DiBattista, adamdibattista@gmail.com

Abstract: This Element addresses the study and documentation of objects made from the durable materials of animal bodies, including bone, antler, ivory, and keratinous tissues. This category of artifacts is common across cultures and regions, yet often escapes close study. The Element aims to be a guide to understanding and documenting worked animal objects for those without a background in zooarchaeology or experience with such artifacts. This Element provides a means of identifying and distinguishing animal materials by emphasizing the value of caution and making full documentation of all observations. Using illustrations and descriptions to help researchers understand the structure of these materials, the volume introduces the terminology and diagnostic factors that differentiate animal materials. It also outlines the techniques craftspeople used to modify animal materials in the past. Finally, this Element presents recording strategies for individuals wishing to study assemblages from archaeological excavations.

Keywords: ivory, worked bone, antler, human–animal studies, zooarchaeology

ISBNs: 9781009532686 (HB), 9781009181679 (PB), 9781009181686 (OC)
ISSNs: 2632-7031 (online), 2632-7023 (print)

Contents

1 Introduction

The use of animal materials is a defining characteristic of human beings. Seventy thousand years ago, early craftspeople at Blombos Cave (located in modern South Africa) created a series of pointed tools from the long bones and mandibles of bovids (likely antelope). The discovery of these tools pushed back the start date for "behavioral modernity," and they demonstrated that the creation of objects from animal bodies is a deeply ancient behavior (Henshilwood et al. 2001). Many years separate us from the humans of Blombos Cave, yet fascination with animal materials remains. In subsequent millennia, humans used bone, antler, ivory, and other animal materials to create a wide variety of material culture. Worked animal objects have continued to play a role in the practices that help to define what it means to be human. We recognize Paleolithic European ivory objects, such as the Venus of Brassempouy and the Lion-man of the Hohlenstein-Stadel, as some of the earliest examples of figural art. The development of writing in Shang dynasty (ca. 1600–1046 BCE) China began with characters inscribed on ox scapulae and turtle plastrons that were transformed and manipulated in a divinatory practice. Important artistic and cultural developments in worked animal materials continued into the modern era. The artisans of Edo-period Japan (1603–1867) transformed the teeth of hippopotami, elephants, boar, and a variety of other animals into intricate *netsuke* carvings. Around the same time, sailors in the Atlantic Ocean began carving scenes of ocean life onto the bones and teeth of whales in a form of art known as scrimshaw.

Creating objects from the bodies of animals is widespread across different cultures, meaning that archaeologists of all subdisciplines and regions must be cognizant of worked animal materials. While many introductions to archaeology highlight ceramic production, lithic production, and metallurgy as major technologies, the production of worked animal objects is rarely addressed despite its cross-cultural prevalence. Instead, these materials are often studied as a subdiscipline of zooarchaeology, or the objects themselves are examined through the lens of art historical analysis. Rather than encompassing only a single craft or medium, the creation of worked animal objects includes a series of related techniques applied to a range of organic materials.

This work represents a reference for those wishing to analyze worked animal objects recovered in archaeological excavations. For the purposes of this Element, the term "worked animal objects" refers to the hard elements of an animal's skeleton that were modified by craftspeople in the past: bone, cartilaginous tissue, antler, dental tissue, and keratinous materials (e.g., horn, baleen, and tortoiseshell). These were not the only animal materials used by humans in the past, as objects like furs, hides, grease, and dung also held significant symbolic, economic, and practical value. However, as these materials were subject to different technological practices and are rare in the archaeological record, they are excluded from this Element. Likewise, modified mollusk shells are not included here, as their shells are significantly different from other animal materials.

Examinations of worked animal objects are strongly guided by the disciplinary backgrounds of the authors who write them. Scholars tend to become familiar with a region or time period, ultimately influencing their understanding of the discipline. Differences in recovery techniques and preservation environments can also impact a scholar's exposure to certain types of worked animal objects, as some materials only survive in arid, frozen, or anaerobic environments. While animal materials are rooted in biological concepts that transcend cultural boundaries, researchers from different backgrounds have varied understandings of these materials. Despite these differences, this Element is an attempt to explore and present a wide range of worked animal materials, so as to be valuable for archaeologists working in any region or time period. Studying objects made from animal materials can be a daunting task without prior experience or zooarchaeological training, so this work emphasizes how thorough recording practices can help researchers better articulate areas of uncertainty. It is the goal of this monograph to aid in identifying animal materials, as well as to help researchers develop a plan for studying and presenting assemblages of worked animal objects.

1.1 History of the Study of Worked Animal Materials

1.1.1 The Identification of Animal Materials

Before there was any formal scientific analysis of animal materials, humans gained experience with the properties of skeletal tissue through enacting technical practices for the creation of worked objects. The formalized scientific study of animal materials has its roots in the Scientific Revolution of the sixteenth and seventeenth centuries. Antonie van Leeuwenhoek, famous for revolutionizing the single-lensed microscope, published observations on the microstructure of bone and tooth. His description and illustration of the structure of elephant ivory notes the similarity of the material to "platted work" and appears to be the earliest depiction of one of the most diagnostic features of proboscidean ivory (van Leeuwenhoek 1678, 1003). By the nineteenth century, biologists, chemists, anatomists, and other researchers were studying the composition of biological organisms on a microscopic level.

Bernhard Schreger (1800) performed some of the early work on the structure of teeth, describing banded growth patterns within enamel. While these patterns are rarely seen within worked animal objects, his line of inquiry was influential for other researchers studying the structure of teeth. Following Schreger, Anders Retzius (1837) was one of the earliest scholars of the microstructure of the teeth of multiple animal species, also observing the distinct crisscrossing bands of elephant tusk that was described by van Leeuwenhoek. Biologist and paleontologist Richard Owen (1856) also identified and illustrated this pattern in proboscidean ivory within his later work *Ivory and the Teeth of Commerce*. In the early nineteenth century, Thomas Franz Hanausek (1907) published comparative studies of the microstructure of a series of animal materials, providing illustrations of features like the dentinal tubules of ivory.

Thomas K. Penniman (1952), the anthropologist and curator of the Pitt-Rivers Museum at the University of Oxford, was one of the first scholars to publish a comparative guide of animal materials using photography, greatly advancing the study of these objects. Since Penniman's work, several journal articles and guides have been published on different aspects of animal material structure. With the ratification of the Convention on International Trade in Endangered Species of Wild Fauna and Flora (CITES) in 1973 and the subsequent bans on elephant ivory, there was a pressing need for government agencies to have a clear means of differentiating animal materials. The CITES identification guides provided further high-quality images and definitions of specific structures within animal teeth.

However, the CITES guides and Penniman's publication show modern animal materials or worked objects in pristine condition, so there have also been several works explicitly aimed at archaeologists and scholars of material culture. Olga Krzyszkowska's (1990) *Ivory and Related Materials* primarily focuses on animal materials found within the Mediterranean region, but her guide to differentiating types of ivory is cited across archaeological subfields. Similarly, Arthur MacGregor (1985) provides a detailed overview of the structure of animal materials, as well as background on the production processes used by craftspeople in the past (especially those in Europe during the post-Roman period). While there is a long history of the study of durable osseous materials, the more ephemeral remains of keratinous materials have not received the same attention. However, since the 1980s, Sonia O'Connor (1987, 2015) has explored methods of identifying archaeological examples of keratinous materials using visual and scientific analysis.

1.1.2 The Study and Interpretation of Worked Animal Objects

As a result of the development of prehistoric archaeology in Europe (specifically France) in the nineteenth century, objects made from animal materials were an important part of early archaeological scholarship. Jacques Boucher de Crèvecœur de Perthes' (1788–1868) discoveries of stone tools in the Somme valley eventually led to the acceptance of his ideas about the age of humanity. Subsequent early scholars inspired by de Perthes, such as Vicomte Alexis de Gourgue and Gabriel de Mortillet, studied the stratigraphic distribution of objects made from animal materials; De Mortillet's (1873, 436) classification of the chronology of the Paleolithic was based, in part, on the presence of bone and antler tools. Opposed to de Mortillet's chronological reasoning, Henri Breuil (1907, see also Davies 2009) also used stratified bone tools as evidence to establish the sequence of the Paleolithic period. By the early twentieth century, the importance of bone tools in the study of the Paleolithic period provided an environment for scholars to produce work focused on tools made from animal materials during this era (e.g., Chauvet 1910).

While research on worked animal materials was becoming more common in the twentieth century, the emphasis on the study of stone tools in prehistoric archaeology resulted in some of the largest theoretical advances. These new perspectives led to a focus on the technological process and detailed typologies of tool types (e.g., Bordes 1961). André Leroi-Gourhan used the study of lithics to develop the idea of the *Chaîne opératoire*, a heuristic that schematizes sequences of technological acts and seeks to reconstruct mental actions and technical gestures related to the purpose of creating, using, and discarding objects (see Sellet 1993). A parallel idea, known as the reduction sequence, was also being developed by American scholars (see Shott 2003). While these ideas were initially applied to stone tools, the *Chaîne opératoire* was subsequently adopted by scholars researching other forms of technology, and it has remained a major influence on the study of worked animal objects.

Important developments in the study of lithics and animal materials also occurred outside France. S.A. Semenov's (1964) research is an example of how the study of lithics and bone and antler tools often occurred in tandem. Semenov originally published *Prehistoric Technology* in Russian in the USSR in 1957, before it was translated into English in 1964. While its reception outside Russian-speaking academic circles was limited, it offered a new methodology focused on recognizing the traces of tool use and understanding the function of tools. Semenov's approach emphasized experimentation as a means of understanding modifications and became the basis for a methodology known as use-wear analysis. Subsequent research on worked animal materials, such as

Douglas Campana's (1989) publication of bone tools from the Zagros and the Levant, explicitly draws on Semenov's approach to use-wear analysis. Since Campana and Semenov's publications, archaeological studies of worked animal objects continue to rely on use-wear analysis by incorporating technologies like SEM microscopy and 3D modeling.

In the 1970s, the study of tools made from osseous materials became a more distinct subfield of prehistoric archaeology, with the first international symposium on prehistoric bone industry organized by Henriette Camps-Fabrer. As a result of these meetings, Camps-Fabrer created the Committee of Nomenclature of Prehistoric Bone Industry, a series that aimed to explore and classify different types of osseous objects (e.g., wind instruments, barbed points, and ornaments), and which led to a series of publications lasting from the 1980s until the 2000s.

Outside of prehistoric archaeology, scholarly emphasis on worked animal materials occurred in countries with long traditions of zooarchaeological research. Working in Hungary, Alice Choyke and László Bartosiewicz researched and published assemblages of worked animal materials originating from a variety of different time periods; their subsequent work also included studies of worked animal objects from other parts of Europe, Anatolia, and the Near East. During the 1990s, Choyke was integral in establishing the study of worked animal objects as a more distinct subfield within archaeology. In 1997, worked animal objects became a focus of the International Council for Archaeozoology (ICAZ), when the inaugural conference of the Worked Bone Research Group (WBRG) was held at the British Museum. Since the second meeting, the WBRG has held biennial conferences in locations around the world, and publications of these proceedings began in 2001. While so much of the previous scholarship on worked animal materials was rooted in specific regions or time periods (often prehistoric Europe), the WBRG represents the work of scholars with different temporal and cultural specializations. In the introduction to the proceedings of the second meeting, Choyke and Bartosiewicz (2001, III) describe the mission of the WBRG, writing that "an effort was made to present these papers on the basis of what *connects* them rather than segregating them by archaeological period or region."

Owing to the focus on tool use in prehistoric archaeology, much of the scholarship on worked animal materials has tried to understand the function of such objects. Methodological studies like use-wear analysis aim to reconstruct how craftspeople used tools in the past. However, major theoretical shifts such as the post-processual critique of New Archaeology have changed how scholars approach material culture. Moreover, zooarchaeology has also begun to move away from interpretations of faunal assemblages that exclusively view the material through a lens of economy and subsistence. As a result, the way scholars approach and present worked animal objects is changing. Recent theoretical perspectives throughout anthropology, archaeology, and the social sciences more generally (e.g., actor-network theory, the ontological turn, materiality studies, human–animal studies, and the incorporation of indigenous perspectives) have begun to influence how scholars think about animal materials (e.g., McNiven 2010; Conneller 2012; Isaakidou 2017).

1.2 Terminology

The study of worked animal materials borrows terminology from the field of zooarchaeology. Like other natural scientists, zooarchaeologists use a specific vocabulary of animal materials within their discipline, allowing researchers to share an understanding of their field of study. Within zooarchaeology, the skeleton is divided into a series of elements, defined as single examples of independent units of the skeleton (e.g., a left humerus, a third molar, and a right mandible) (Reitz & Wing 1999, 9). Zooarchaeologists also identify the side of an element, often by orienting it into its proper anatomical position. This allows researchers to talk about specific regions of the element using anatomical terms of location, such as proximal, distal, medial, and lateral.

Describing an element as "proximal" indicates it is located closer to the center of the body, whereas distal means the opposite. For example, the head of the femur (i.e., the part of the bone that articulates with the pelvis) is the proximal end, while the area closest to the patella is the distal end. A human's fingers are distal to the elbow because they are farther from the center of the body. "Medial" and "lateral" are terms describing the proximity to the midline, an imaginary line along the center that splits the body into left and right sides. The surface of an element closer to the midline is the "medial" side, while the "lateral" side is farther. For example, the fibula articulates with the lateral surface of the tibia. There are a specific set of locational terms (e.g., lingual, labial, and occlusal) to describe teeth, although the terms proximal and distal are still applicable. Likewise, the bases of antlers and horns are proximal, while the ends are distal.

In addition to anatomical terms of location, skeletal elements can also be understood in terms of planes that "transect" the materials. The transverse plane runs perpendicular to the proximal–distal axis, meaning that a transverse cut across the bone would separate the proximal and distal ends. Cutting a long bone across the transverse plane results in a cut surface appearing as an elliptical cross section (e.g., the diameter of the shaft, Figure 1). Skeletal elements can also be transected along the longitudinal plane, parallel to the proximal–distal

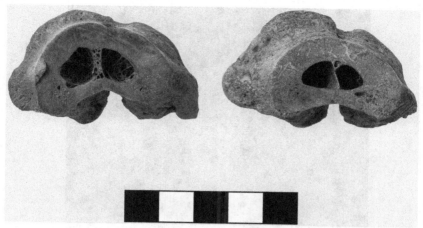

Figure 1 Sawed metapodial ends from cattle from ancient Methone
(ca. 700 BCE).
Source: Photograph by Jeff Vanderpool.

axis. Cutting a bone along the longitudinal plane would result in two halves, both preserving the proximal and distal ends; the cut surfaces would encompass the entire length of the bone. These planes offer a means of conceptualizing the position of worked animal objects within the materials from which they originated. Moreover, there are biological features within animal materials with specific orientations (e.g., the osteonic canal system), meaning certain diagnostic aspects of animal materials may only be visible within a transverse or longitudinal view.

2 Bone and Antler

Bone is a hard tissue composed of roughly ~60 percent inorganic components (primarily calcium hydroxyapatite) and ~40 percent organic components (collagen and other proteins). At the visible scale, this material forms in two different structural orientations: cortical and trabecular bone. Cortical bone, sometimes called compact bone, is a dense structure that makes up most of the strength-bearing portions of the skeleton. It has a grainy appearance resulting from cellular processes involved in the remodeling of the bone. Specialized cells create a system of cavities which supply the bone with nutrients. These cavities are surrounded by concentric layers of bone, resulting in a circular structure known as the osteon. This network of cavities and circular growth is just visible to the naked eye, giving bone its textured appearance (Figures 2, bottom detail and 3, bottom detail). These cavities are part of an osteonic network that includes Haversian canals and Volkmann's canals. Haversian canals run lengthwise, while Volkmann's canals are oriented perpendicular to the

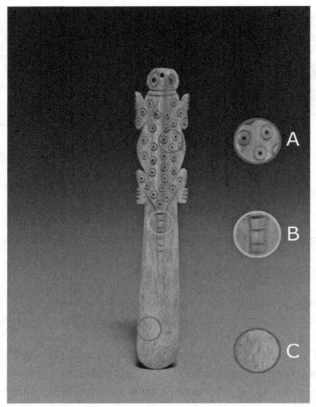

Figure 2 Andean bone spatula in the Nasca style (100 BCE–700 CE) showing the ring-and-dot motif (top detail, incised lines (central detail), and the osteonic canal systems present in bone (bottom detail).

Source: Cleveland Museum of Art, accession number: 1955.83.

Haversian system. It is easier to observe the osteonic structure of bone under magnification, and the presence of this feature serves as an important diagnostic for determining whether an object is made from bone.

Trabecular (also known as cancellous) bone is a porous or "spongy" structure that is markedly less dense than cortical bone. Made up of a series of open struts (trabeculae), trabecular bone provides the skeletal element with support and flexibility. This tissue is primarily located within the ends of skeletal elements (e.g., the head of a femur), as well as within vertebrae, ribs, and other flat bones. The distinct open structure of trabecular bone is highly recognizable, but not as widely used as a medium for carving; regardless, objects made from trabecular bone have been found in archaeological contexts. The porosity of trabecular bone makes it more likely to degrade in adverse preservation environments, so this material may also be underrepresented within the archaeological record.

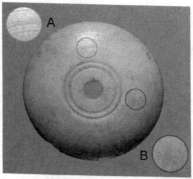

Figure 3 Bone spindle whorl from Iran (Early Islamic Period, eighth–tenth centuries CE). (A) Shows striations from lathe turning. (B) Shows osteonic canals.

Source: Cleveland Museum of Art, accession number: 1963.645.

2.1 Skeletal Elements

Owing to its wide availability and structural variation, bone is one of the most common animal materials used for the creation of material culture. Many skeletal elements are composed of bone, and their morphology and structure (i.e., composition of trabecular and cortical bone) can vary considerably. Individuals in the past may have favored certain types of bones for their strength and abundance of cortical tissue (e.g., long bones or metapodials), as some of these elements provide solid portions of carvable material. While certain elements offer more practical advantages, humans in the past also relied on skeletal elements for less obvious reasons. For example, individuals among several cultural groups (e.g., indigenous Americans and groups living in central Asia and Western Europe) took advantage of the uniquely flat properties of the scapula within a set of divinatory practices known as scapulimancy (Tanner 1978; Sayers 1992; Nishida 2016). The choice to utilize a given skeletal element is rooted in the social and cultural environment of technological practice. While certain skeletal elements were undoubtedly more commonly used by craftspeople in the past, humans created material culture from nearly every type of bone.

Zooarchaeologists and other scholars of anatomy subdivide skeletal elements into several categories (Table 1). While certain scholarly fields may class elements differently (e.g., osteologists group human metacarpals and phalanges as long bones), the following elements are grouped with respect to the study of worked bone objects (Figure 4).

Table 1 Types of skeletal elements

Long bones	Humerus, radius, ulna, femur, tibia, fibula
Metapodials	Metacarpus, metatarsus
Flat bones	Scapula, ribs, pelvis
Axial skeleton	Vertebrae
Carpals, tarsals, and sesamoids	Patella, astragalus
Bones of the skull	Mandible, cranial
Phalanges	1st, 2nd, 3rd Phalanges

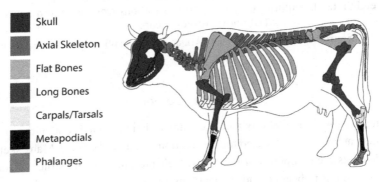

Figure 4 Skeletal elements of a cow.
Source: Drawing by Leah Olson.

2.1.1 Long Bones

Among most animals, long bones are typified by a hollow shaft (diaphysis) surrounded by cortical bone, with two ends (epiphyses) mostly made up of spongy, trabecular bone. Long bones store marrow within the diaphysis in a structure known as the "medullary cavity." When cut transversely, long bones show the medullary cavity as a hollow portion (Figure 5). Four long bones (humerus, femur, tibia, and radius) bear a significant portion of the animal's weight, are critical for movement, and are generally thicker and stronger than other elements. The concentration of dense cortical bone, as well as the regular shape, made long bones an appealing material for craftspeople. The tubular structure of long bones was well-suited to objects like musical instruments, tool handles, rings, and pyxides. Additionally, the long, straight sections of cortical tissue contained within long bones allowed for the creation of objects like points, needles, and spoons.

Craftspeople often removed the epiphyses and altered the shape of the diaphysis, making identification of the specific element or species exceptionally

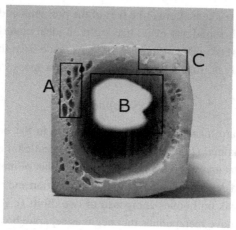

Figure 5 View of the transverse surface of an object made from a ruminant metapodial from the site of Hasanlu in Iran (ca. ninth century BCE). (A) Trabecular bone; (B) typical shape of a ruminant metapodial; and (C) cortical bone.

Source: Metropolitan Museum of Art, accession number: 60.20.27.

difficult. However, regions of certain long bones can be diagnostic and identifiable. In many taxa, the proximal shaft of the tibia appears triangular in cross section. The diaphysis of the humerus tends to be thicker than other long bones, which may aid in identification. The fibula and ulna are narrower than the other long bones, resulting in the use of these elements for objects like awls or small points. The ulna articulates with the radius and humerus within the forelimb of the animal, and its shape naturally tapers toward a pointed distal end (known as the styloid process). As a result, craftspeople often modified the distal ends of the ulna to create pointed tools. Fibulae are fairly variable among different species and can be nearly absent or much smaller than the other long bones. In bovines, the fibula exists only as a small region of bone fused to the proximal and distal ends of the tibia. Equids possess a fibula that is shorter than the tibia, while the fibula is robust among pigs and other suids. Owing to the slender shape of this skeletal element, examples of needles and other thin points made from fibulae are known throughout the world. Points made from pig fibulae are relatively common in European assemblages, but fibula from very different species have been used for similar tools as well; there is an Australian tradition of creating points from kangaroo fibulae that began in the Pleistocene era (Langley et al. 2016).

Long bone shafts were a rich source of material for worked animal objects, but craftspeople also made use of the proximal and distal ends as well. For example, the head of the humerus (the part of the proximal end that articulates with the scapula) is round and even, making it an ideal material for an object like a spindle whorl (Arabatzis 2016). As objects made from the epiphyses are composed primarily of trabecular bone, they exhibit a spongy appearance.

2.1.2 Metapodials

The metapodials are located immediately proximal to the bones making up the digits of the animal (Figure 6); these bones are called metacarpals in the forelimbs and metatarsals in the hindlimbs. The number of metapodials differs among species and depends on the method of locomotion and number of digits. Ruminants that walk on hooves composed of two digits (e.g., cattle, cervids, sheep, and goats) have metapodials that begin as separate bones and fuse during infancy. Animals that have hooves composed of a single digit (e.g., equids) have one metapodial that bears the weight of the animal and is similarly robust. However, equids also have smaller, styloid-shaped metapodials (often called "splint bones") that are located on both sides of the weight-bearing metapodial. The morphology and size of metapodials differ among animals that walk on their toes or on the soles of their feet. These species generally have more digits, corresponding to greater numbers of smaller sized metapodials. Despite the small size, there are examples of worked objects made from the metapodials of these species (Choyke et al. 2004, 187, fig 18; Luik 2012, 95, see fig. 4.3).

The metapodials of ruminants and equids have served as popular elements for creating worked objects across different cultures and time periods for several reasons (see Schibler 1981, 21; Zhilin 1998; Schibler 2012, 341;

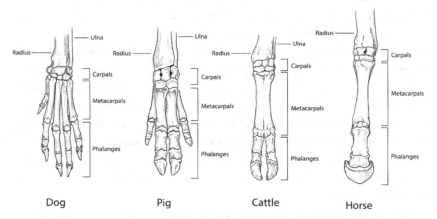

Figure 6 Forelimbs of mammals with different numbers of digits.
Source: Drawing by Leah Olson, after (Reitz & Wing 1999, 59, fig. 3.14).

Choyke & Tóth 2013, 339). Like long bones, these bones are also exceptionally thick and straight, offering large portions of cortical bone that can be turned into a variety of objects. The fusion process leaves behind a channel following the length of the bone (*sulcus*) which provided craftspeople a means of splitting the bone along the longitudinal axis (see Section "Splitting Techniques"). The smaller metapodials of equids (i.e., splints) have much less bone, but craftspeople could use them to create points (Russell 2005, 341, fig. 16.2). Additionally, the metapodials are generally regarded as contributing less to the diet than other elements because there is very little meat surrounding these bones, often leading to them being discarded. However, the parts of the animal considered appealing or useful in dietary practices are socially constructed, and metapodials can be a valuable source of marrow. As a result, the relationship between the dietary value of an element and its use as a raw material may not be the same in all cultures.

Identifying the elements used to create a worked bone object can often be difficult, but recognizing examples of worked ruminant metapodials is possible due to the distinct morphology of the bones. The initial fusion of the metapodials results in a bifurcated appearance visible in cross section; in transverse cross sections nearer to the proximal and distal ends, the metapodial appears separated by a thin portion of bone (Figure 1). In examples of worked animal objects where the interior of the diaphysis is unaltered, the remains of the fusion process may offer clear evidence for the use of a ruminant metapodial.

2.1.3 Flat Bones

Composed of a thin layer of cortical bone surrounding a core of trabecular bone, flat bones include the ribs, the scapula, the bones of the pelvis, and a number of the bones of the cranium (classified separately here). Worked examples of the ribs and scapula are found more commonly in the archaeological record, while examples of modified pelvis bones are comparatively rare. The ribs of many mammals are relatively flat, making them an ideal material for an implement like a spatula, scraper, thresher, or similar tool. Craftspeople also used a longitudinal splitting technique to create tool handles by separating the rib into two halves and attaching the bones to a metal or stone implement (Hamilton & Nicholson 2007).

The scapula resembles a rough triangle and is so thin in certain species that it appears partially translucent. Owing to its unique shape, the scapula had many uses in the ancient world: scapulimancy (see Section "Flat Bones"), digging implements (Xie et al. 2017), threshing tools (Medina et al. 2018), and hide and fiber processing tools (Hofman 1980). Incised scapulae have also been found throughout the ancient Near East and Anatolia, and while the interpretation of these artifacts varies, it is thought that they may have functioned as musical instruments (Zukerman et al. 2007; Koitabashi 2013). The scapulae of larger animals could also be useful in the production of other objects: A whale scapula recovered from a well in the Athenian Agora exhibited use wear, indicating it was used as a working surface (Papadopoulos & Ruscillo 2002) and mammoth scapulae found at the Kostyonki–Borshchyovo archaeological complex were dug into the ground and used as surfaces for craft production (Semenov 1964, 171, fig. 87).

2.1.4 Axial Skeleton

The axial skeleton (i.e., the spine) is made up of several types of vertebral bones. The two bones closest to the cranium are known as the atlas and axis, which provide support for the skull. Following these elements are a series of different types of vertebrae: cervical, thoracic, lumbar, sacral, and caudal. Vertebrae have a high proportion of trabecular bone, as well as thin and breakable sections. Additionally, butchering practices often split or break vertebrae. For these reasons, the vertebrae of most mammals were not commonly used by craftspeople, although there are modified examples thought to be early expressions of symbolic thought (Majkić et al. 2018; Ardelean et al. 2023). The vertebrae of larger animals served as a valuable material for a variety of cultures. A bowl made from a whale vertebra was found at the Neolithic site of Skara Brae (Orkney Islands of Scotland; Childe et al. 1929, 274, fig. 34). Similarly, minimally modified whale vertebrae were found at the Phoenician colony of Motya on Sicily (ca. sixth–fifth century BCE) in association with *Murex* shells, suggesting that these bones were used as a working surface for dye production (Reese 2005). While worked mammalian vertebrae are generally rare, the vertebrae of fish and sharks were commonly used to create objects like beads (see Section "Fish Bone and Cartilage").

2.1.5 Sesamoids, Carpals, and Tarsals

These elements are grouped together because they are small, and worked examples are rare within the archaeological record. The limited recovery of such objects may be a function of practical or cultural selection processes that did not favor the use of small bones encased in connective tissue. Additionally, factors related to taphonomy, preservation, and excavation methods may also bias against the recovery of these smaller elements. Sesamoids are spherical bones located within tendons, the largest of which is the patella. There is little evidence for the modification of sesamoids beyond that of the patella (Hahn 1972, 260–263).

Carpals are a collection of small bones located between the metacarpals and the radius/ulna, while tarsals are found between the metatarsals and the tibia/fibula. Like sesamoids, worked carpals and tarsals are rare apart from one large tarsal bone: the astragalus. The astragalus is roughly rectangular in shape, with four faces that are similar in size. The bone can be thrown like a die and land on one of its four sides. As a result, the astragalus was used as a gaming piece, as well as a divination tool for astragalomancy. These properties make the astragalus one of the most widely studied and common worked animal objects across cultures and time periods (Gilmour 1997; Affanni 2008; Carè 2025). The astragalus is colloquially known as a "knucklebone," most often in reference to its use in games; certain publications continue to use this term. Semenov (1964, 175–176) notes that carpals and tarsals of mammoths found at Mousterian-period Kosh-Koba in Crimea were used as anvils for craft production. Examples of worked carpals and tarsals from smaller species are significantly rarer, although an example of a worked carpal or tarsal of a turtle was found in a midden in south Florida (Walker 1992, 239, fig. 12).

2.1.6 Bones of the Skull

The skull is made up of the mandible and a series of fused elements of the cranium, including the frontal, parietal, and occipital bones. The cranial bones can be oddly shaped, irregular, and difficult to separate, potentially making them a less desirable material for craftspeople. Nevertheless, examples of worked cranial bone are found within the archaeological record (Boardman 1967, 211, no. 600, pl. 97). Additionally, the medieval trade in walrus ivory spawned an artistic practice of carving the part of the animal's skull known as the rostrum (maxilla, frontal, and nasal bones). Mandibles, especially those of large animals, were more commonly used within the creation of worked animal objects (Barrett et al. 2022). For example, cattle mandibles were used as smoothing tools at Middle Bronze Age sites in Hungary (Choyke & Schibler 2007, 59–60). The ramus (the region of the mandible between the teeth and the rest of the skull) provides a flat surface that was also used by craftspeople wishing to make items like discs or buttons (MacGregor 1985, 61, fig. 36; Klippel & Price 2007, 111, fig. 10).

2.1.7 Phalanges

The phalanges are the bones that make up an animal's digits (e.g., fingers, hoofs, and flippers). Like long bones, most phalanges have proximal and distal ends and a small diaphysis in the center, although the distal phalanges (equivalent to the tip of the finger or the toe) usually come to a more pointed end because they do not articulate with any other bones. Distal phalanges can also be covered in a keratinous plate (i.e., fingernail), hoof, or claw. One of the most common modifications of phalanges is the creation of claw pendants; craftspeople who made such pendants often created a suspension hole through the proximal end of the distal (usually third) phalanx, which was often still attached to the keratinous portion. As keratin is highly susceptible to decomposition (see Section 4), usually only the modified bone preserves. In addition to claw pendants, there are several examples of worked phalanges in archaeological contexts that were seemingly chosen for the unique shape of the bone and appear to have symbolic uses (Pawłowska & Barański 2020, 8; Leder et al. 2021). Additionally, there are also examples of worked phalanges that have ambiguous functions and often referred to as "toggles" (St-Pierre et al. 2021, 241). It is likely that some worked phalanges actually functioned as clothing fasteners, while others may have been gaming pieces (e.g., Bläuer et al. 2019) or other types of objects.

2.2 Other Types of Bone

While studies of worked bone often focus on objects made from a limited number of medium and large terrestrial mammals (e.g., cattle, equids, cervids, camelids, and ovicaprids), craftspeople also made objects from the bones of birds, fish, reptiles, and marine mammals. The choice of these bones was likely guided by the practical advantages of these materials, as well as symbolic associations that gave them value.

2.2.1 Avian Bones

Due to the requirements of flying and the unique morphology of avian species, the bones of birds differ from those of mammals in several ways. Birds possess some skeletal elements which are absent in mammals. These differences are especially prevalent in relation to the elements located in the wings and feet; birds possess different forms of metacarpals, metatarsals, carpals, and tarsals. While this may seem like a minor distinction, certain cultural groups used these unique bones to create worked objects. Cultural groups on New Guinea often used the tibiotarsus and the tarsometatarsus (akin to a tibia and metatarsus) of the cassowary bird to create daggers (Dominy et al. 2018). Some of the skeletal elements shared by birds and mammals are also morphologically different. The proximal end of an avian humerus is relatively flat and elliptical, hardly resembling the comparable structure in mammals. Additionally, relative size of certain elements may differ between birds and mammals; for example, the avian sternum is comparatively larger than the same element in mammals.

The inner structure of this type of bone represents one of the most consequential differences between mammalian and avian species. It is often said that bird bones are hollow, and thus lighter to assist with flight. It is more accurate to describe bird bones as covered in a thin layer of cortical bone, with concentrations of trabecular bone at the ends. Avian trabecular bone is markedly more open than that of mammalian bone, with large hollow pockets. The shafts of avian bones are the hollowest portions, with "struts" of trabecular bone which form intermittently throughout. These features make avian bones feel significantly lighter and more delicate than other mammalian bones. These features made them appealing to craftspeople for specific uses (e.g., the creation of musical instruments). Objects made from the birds of bones should feel lighter than objects made from mammalian bones of a comparable size. However, there are a host of taphonomic processes that contribute to demineralization and degradation of mammalian bones. Therefore, the most effective way to recognize worked animal objects made from bird bones is to develop a general understanding of avian skeletal anatomy.

2.2.2 Turtle Shell (Carapace and Plastron)

The shell of the turtle (reptiles from order *testudines* including terrapins, tortoises, and sea turtles) is an osseous structure covered in keratinous scales called "scutes." The top of the shell is called the carapace, while the bottom is known as the plastron. "Turtle shell" should not be confused with "tortoiseshell," the name given to a keratinous material made from the scutes of sea turtles (see Section 4.3). Turtle shell is akin to flat bone, as it has a trabecular core surrounded by two layers of cortical bone. Additionally, the elements of the turtle shell are joined together "at soft unmineralized collagen sutures" (Achrai & Wagner 2013, 5891). Craftspeople using turtle shells took advantage of its shape to create rounded objects that incorporated this structure. Archaeological examples of musical instruments made from turtle shells (e.g., rattles) have been found across the United States (Gillreath-Brown 2019). Similarly, the ancient Greek lyre (*chelys*) was made from a turtle shell, examples of which have been found in several archaeological contexts (e.g., Kokkoliou 2020). There is also some evidence for craftspeople carving smaller pieces of turtle shell to create implements or tools (e.g., Hull 2018, 945, fig. 16). Pieces of the carapace and plastron are easy to identify within archaeological assemblages because they feature prominent suture lines. The shell frequently breaks along these sutures, resulting in rectangular or hexagonal pieces surrounded by wavy, jagged edges. Due to the suture lines, shell is often mistaken for cranial bones of humans or other mammals. However, turtle shell has a heavily ridged exterior which is rougher than cranial bone.

2.2.3 Marine Mammal Bones

The exploitation of marine resources, whether through hunting or scavenging, has afforded humans access to the skeletal material of marine mammals. Owing to the requirements of swimming in a saline environment, marine mammals evolved to have denser bones than those of terrestrial mammals, making them an appealing material for craftspeople. As whale habitats are widely distributed across the major oceans, these animals have served as important resources (e.g., meat, oil, and bones) for a variety of cultures around the world. Whale bone served as a particularly useful material for craftspeople in the past. It should be noted that the "whale bone" under consideration is separate from the keratinous material baleen, which is sometimes referred to as "whalebone" (see Section 4.2). The earliest evidence for the modification of whale bones comes from Upper Paleolithic period sites in the northern Pyrenees (Pétillon 2013), and the practice of carving whale bones continued into the modern era with the development of scrimshaw in the eighteenth and nineteenth centuries. Craftspeople often sought out the flat, dense sections of the mandible (referred to as the "pan bone"); the large size and uniquely flat shape of these sections of the jawbone makes objects made from this section of the skeleton identifiable as whale bone. Owing to the immense size of whales, craftspeople also had the ability to carve large sections of whale bone without leaving features to identify a particular skeletal element. Nevertheless, it is often possible to identify whale bone owing to the unique morphological properties of the material.

Whale bone is composed primarily of trabecular tissue, surrounded by a thin layer of cortical bone. Unlike the bones of other mammals, whale bones lack a medullary cavity, meaning that there is no hollow section that the craftsperson had to incorporate in their carvings. This material afforded craftspeople the opportunity to create large objects, carving every surface without having any hollow sections. The size of the bones, combined with the lack of medullary cavity, can make whale bone relatively easy to recognize after it has been modified. Additionally, trabecular whale bone looks different than either the trabecular or cortical bone of terrestrial mammals. Trabecular whale bone has a dense appearance similar to the cortical bone of terrestrial mammals; however, it is speckled with trabeculae that are not overly clustered. The overall appearance is that of markedly grainy cortical bone. Crucially, the trabecular bone is remarkably homogeneous throughout the skeleton. Jean-Marc Pétillon (2013, 528) describes the structure of whale bone, writing: "[W]ith few exceptions, the trabeculae are rather evenly distributed, and they never indicate a 'spongy' side or end opposed to a 'compact' one; they can be seen on all sides of the objects and across their entire length." Certain elements are an exception, as the ribs and vertebrae of whales exhibit more concentrated areas of trabeculae that appear similar to the same elements in terrestrial mammals. Moreover, objects made of whale bone may still intersect both the outer cortical layer and the inner trabecular tissue, resulting in a more heterogeneous appearance overall. In addition to whales, there is also archaeological evidence for the modification of the bones of bottlenose dolphins (van den Hurk et al. 2023, 148) and walruses (Barrett et al. 2022). The bones of these species exhibit similar features, which can complicate the differentiation among marine mammal skeletal materials.

2.2.4 Fish Bone and Cartilage

The skeletons of bony fishes (*osteichthyes*) are made up of a set of cranial (larger and more diagnostic) and axial bones (smaller vertebrae and spines). The bones of fish differ from those of mammals, reptiles, and birds, making it easy to differentiate them within the faunal assemblage. The cranial bones are relatively flat, such that they often exhibit a degree of translucency, and the vertebrae of the axial skeleton are round with spiny processes. Cartilaginous fish (*Chondrichthyes*) exhibit similar anatomy, but the skeletal elements are made up of cartilage rather than bone.

There are many barriers to the identification of fish remains: The preservation of fish bones is highly dependent on the conditions of the burial environment, and systematic studies necessitate proper recovery techniques (e.g., sieving and flotation). These factors similarly impact the recovery of worked animal objects made from the bodies of fish. As a result of these factors, fish bone artifacts appear to be less common than other types of worked animal objects, although it is unlikely that the rarity of these objects is a result of issues of preservation and recovery alone. The remains of fish were unlikely to have been a favored material for craftspeople in the past, as the bones are generally small and brittle, making modifications difficult.

Regardless, craftspeople still created a range of objects from different skeletal elements of bony and cartilaginous fish. In many cases, craftspeople created objects from the skeletons of fish by making only small modifications to an element. The vertebrae of fish served as a popular material for the creation of beads and other similar objects because the central portion of this element is exceptionally round and relatively easy to perforate; fish vertebrae are so naturally even that unworked examples are often mistaken for finished objects. Similarly, the fin spines of certain types of fish (e.g., catfish) offered craftspeople a naturally serrated point that could be modified into a tool (e.g., Hull 2018, 945, fig. 16). A similar approach was used for the non-bone elements of cartilaginous fish; stingray spines are naturally blade-like extensions of the skeleton which held high symbolic value in certain cultures (Haines et al. 2008) and were sometimes worked to create points or blades (e.g., Wake 2001, 187, fig. 9.5). Additionally, certain fish possess a set of teeth that sits within a part of the lower jaw called the pharyngeal plate. These teeth are denser than fish bone, and are composed of enamel and dentine like the teeth of mammals. Pharyngeal teeth could be lightly modified and worn as a form of adornment, with evidence for this practice found in Mesolithic sites in the Upper and Lower Danube regions (Cristiani et al. 2014, 304).

In addition to this technological approach, in which craftspeople adapted the natural shape of the skeletal element to create an object that was similar in shape, there are also instances of craftspeople making significant modifications to fish bones: A chess piece carved from the cranial bone (cleithrum) of a haddock was found at Siglunes in Iceland (Lárusdóttir et al. 2012, 22). Additionally, species of sturgeon have rows of bony scales known as scutes that were also modified by craftspeople; archaeological examples have been found in Estonia (Jonuks & Rannamäe 2018, 170. fig. 12.3). Scutes generally have a diamond or kite shape, with an underside that resembles trabecular bone.

2.3 Antler

Antler is a branched bony structure that grows from the skulls of animals in the cervidae family (e.g., deer, elk, reindeer, caribou, and moose). With the exception of reindeer, only male cervids possess antlers, and the structures are shed and regrown seasonally in conjunction with changes in testosterone. Most male cervids (stags) grow antlers during an infertile period between spring and summer, when the structures become covered in a thin layer of velvet. At the end of summer, stags begin to secrete more testosterone in advance of the mating season. With the rise of testosterone, stags will lose their velvet and the antlers will begin a process of ossification and solidification. By the winter, testosterone levels drop, and the stags will cast off their antlers. Antler can be acquired by either hunting cervids or collecting sheds from the landscape. Shed antler is a source of nutrients for many animals (e.g., squirrels, porcupines, mice, and even the deer themselves), so this material needs to be collected shortly after it is cast.

These hormonal changes affect several aspects of the appearance and structure of the antler. The periosteum (the exterior layer of thick vascular tissue beneath the velvet) has a distinctly ridged and knobbed appearance resulting from these seasonal processes. The outer surface of antler often displays a series of channels running parallel to the length of the appendage; the appearance of the outer surface is shaped by blood vessels underlying the velvet, which alters the blood flow in accordance with hormonal and seasonal changes

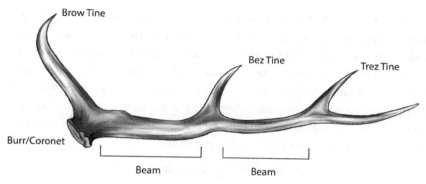

Figure 7 Structure of the antler.
Source: Drawing by Leah Olson.

(Goss 1983, 160–164, figs. 7–8). The surface of antler can have different textures, as the antler of some species (e.g., red deer and white-tailed deer) exhibits a globular appearance known as "pearlation." While the outer surface is clearly distinguishable from skeletal bone, it is also likely to have been removed by craftspeople.

Antlers develop from permanent outgrowths on the cranium known as the pedicles. The region where the antler meets the pedicle is called the coronet or burr, and the main branch extending from the coronet is called the beam. At different locations along the beam, the antler branches into points known as tines. The arrangement and number of tines is dependent on the species of deer, although the first three tines are called the brow, the bez, and the trez tines (Figure 7). Among certain species (e.g., red deer), the beam terminates into a series of forked tines known as the crown. Fallow deer (*Cervus elaphus*) only have brow and bez tines, but the top part of the beam extends into a large, flattened area known as "palmation." While is impossible to determine whether significantly modified antler objects were the result of hunting or collection, antler objects that preserve the coronet can show evidence that the antler was shed. A smooth coronet without any pieces of the pedicle is an indication that the antler was not cut or broken from the cranium, and was therefore shed.

The creation of antler objects began in the Paleolithic, where it was a crucial material for tools like points, harpoons, and hammers. It also served as a medium for artistic representation, such as the representation of a bison licking an insect bite that adorned a spear-thrower found at the Upper Paleolithic site of Abri de la Madeleine in France (Paillet 1999, 292, fig. 351). Likewise, antler was a important material for tools throughout many Neolithic cultures in Europe and Asia. In Bronze Age Eurasia, antler played a crucial role in horse-riding activities, as it was used for bits and cheek pieces

(Chechushkov et al. 2018). In the Pre-European Southeastern United States, white-tailed deer had significant symbolic meaning for the Cherokee; antler objects found in sites from the Mississippian and early Historic periods (800–1600 CE) help demonstrate the importance of the human–deer relationship (Peres & Altman 2018). Antler was also a material of major importance in Northern Europe and Scandinavia beginning in the tenth century CE: Antler combs from this region became particularly important aspects of material culture that had strong social and economic value.

2.4 Differentiating Bone and Antler

Differentiating substantially modified bone and antler objects can be challenging, as both materials have similar compositions and appearances. Understanding the differences in the shape and internal composition of both materials aids the identification process. Researchers need to be able to hypothesize how an object was originally oriented within the animal material, asking the question: "Is it possible for this material to have been made from antler or bone based on its size and structure?"

In addition to understanding the shape and structure of these animal materials, observing the surface can also aid in the identification process. The outer surface of completely unmodified antler appears creased, wrinkled, ridged, or pearlated, markedly different from the generally smooth appearance of bone (Figure 8A). While modifications can remove a portion of the outer surface, aspects of this texture may remain subtly visible (Figure 9). Antler also appears

Figure 8 Antler object from ancient Methone (ca. 700 BCE) showing exterior surface (A) and trabecular tissue on the underside (B).
Source: Photograph by Jeff Vanderpool.

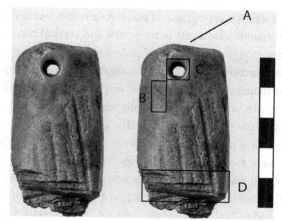

Figure 9 Antler object with hack marks from ancient Methone (ca. 700 BCE).

Source: Photograph by Jeff Vanderpool.

Figure 10 Antler object showing cut transverse surface from ancient Methone (ca. 700 BCE).

Source: Photo by Jeff Vanderpool.

distinct from bone in cross section: The interior of antler is made up of two types of osseous tissue. Beneath the outer surface of the antler is a layer of thick cortical tissue that transitions to a core of densely packed trabecular (spongy) tissue. The outer edge of antler tends to be wavy, surrounding a layer of dense cortical tissue. The cortical tissue transitions into a central portion of spongy trabecular tissue, which is at its most porous in the center. Unlike bone, the interior portion of antler lacks a medullary cavity and is composed entirely of trabecular tissue (Figure 10). The solid interior structure of antler is one of the easiest ways to identify the material.

Within skeletal bone, the location of trabecular tissue is generally confined to certain portions of the element (e.g., the head of the femur), and it is covered by only a thin layer of cortical bone. As a result, worked bone objects rarely exhibit perpendicular layers of trabecular and cortical bone. Conversely, objects made from longitudinal slices of antler will likely capture some portion of the trabecular structure. Cortical tissue along the length of the object, coupled with trabecular material on the underside, might suggest that the material is antler; however, ribs which have been split longitudinally can appear similar to longitudnal sections of antler. Additionally, worked bone objects made from the epiphyses of long bones will prominently display trabecular bone, potentially making them resemble antler. When differentiating bone from antler, researchers need to take multiple criteria into account, including the appearance of the trabecular tissue itself. MacGregor (1985, 12) identifies trabecular antler as composed of "unbroken canals" that are "immediately distinguishable from the more discrete formations found in skeletal bones." The trabeculae of antler generally appear more ordered than those of bone, with longer canal-like sections (Figure 8B). However, trabecular antler and trabecular bone can still look similar, especially in specimens that are degraded.

The lack of medullary cavity, combined with a dense trabecular section, is a strong indication that the material is antler. Yet antler is generally more prone to degradation than bone, and the outer cortical layer may survive better than the inner trabecular tissue. Craftspeople may have also removed the internal trabecular section to create objects like hafts or handles, so it is possible for antler objects to imitate the hollow structure of long bones. As a result, the lack of interior trabecular tissue should not necessarily be a disqualifying factor when considering whether an object is made from antler.

FACTORS TO CONSIDER

General Shape: Does the shape of the object retain any forked triangular sections characteristic of antler? If the object under consideration is particularly long, does its length make it more likely to have been created from antler?

Outer Appearance: If the outer surface can be recognized, and it has not been substantially modified, does it look smooth (bone) or ridged (antler)?

Inner Appearance: Is there an indication of a hollow interior section corresponding to a medullary cavity (bone) or is there more dense trabecular tissue (antler)?

Pitfalls and Possible Misidentifications: An object exhibiting dense trabeculae is likely to be antler, but consider whether other materials are possible (e.g., whale bone) or whether it could have been made from an area of trabecular bone (e.g., epiphysis). If an object has cortical tissue overlying a consistent layer of trabecular tissue, consider whether it could be made from a rib.

3 Ivory and Animal Teeth

The processes of natural selection have resulted in teeth evolved to serve many different functions. The morphology of these structures can differ immensely, but certain aspects of tooth structure are shared across species. Teeth are comprised of two main parts: the root and the crown. The root extends into the bones of the mandible or maxilla, while the crown represents the visible portion of the tooth. Teeth are usually divided into four classes: molars, premolars, canines, and incisors. Canines or incisors most often serve as a source for worked animal objects, as these teeth can be larger or more prominent than the molars and premolars. Additionally, teeth are composed of several types of tissue: cementum, dentine, enamel, and pulp.

3.1 Cementum

Cementum (sometimes called cement) is a hard tissue that covers the roots of teeth, helping them to remain stable within the bone. However, cementum can also cover large portions of the exposed tooth, such as in the incisors of proboscideans. It is a softer material than dentine, with less mineralized inorganic material (~45 percent). The exterior surface of cementum may be a rougher surface than dentine or enamel, although it can also appear fairly smooth. Within the interior section of the tooth, these materials meet at a region known as the cementum-dentine junction. The appearance of this region varies between species, making it a potentially useful criterion for characterizing ivory objects.

3.2 Dentine

Most of the tooth is composed of dentine, a composite of inorganic crystalized apatite and an organic matrix of collagen. The collagen matrix contains a network of dentinal tubules, cylindrical structures with hollow cores (~5 μm in diameter). The arrangement of these tubules differs among species and even between tooth types within the same species. For example, the orientation of dentinal tubules in hippopotamus canines differs from those within hippopotamus incisors. As one of the most basic units of dentine microstructure, the orientation of the tubules forms the basis for the larger diagnostic patterns within different types of ivory (e.g., the Schreger pattern).

As dentine is continuously generated, many teeth used for ivory show visible signs of the growth process through a sequence of growth layers within the tooth. These layers, called lamellae, are often visible, form in predictable ways, and provide a means of characterizing the material. In addition to the growth layers, many teeth exhibit visually distinct areas where the new dentine is formed in the center of the tooth, distal to the pulp cavity. This region, called the "Interstitial Zone" or "TIZ" by Espinoza and Mann (1992, see also the updated CITES guide: Baker et al. 2020) appears as a heterogenous dark line or arc within the teeth of hippopotami and suids.

Dentine also provides the basis for the definition of the term "ivory," although different cultural understandings of the word have caused debate over which materials actually qualify. Some argue that only objects made from the dentine of elephant tusks should be called ivory, while others widen that definition to include teeth belonging to a variety of species. For the purposes of this work, the term ivory is applied to animals with teeth containing large amounts of dentine that can be substantially carved, namely: proboscideans (i.e., elephant and its extinct relatives), hippopotami, suids (e.g., warthog, boar, and pig), walruses, narwhals, toothed whales, and dugongids. While dentine varies considerably, the material has some general features shared across species. Lacking the osteonic and haversian canal systems, it is both denser and more homogeneous than bony materials.

3.2.1 Color

The word "ivory" is synonymous with a creamy shade of white typical of the material when it is fresh, yet a variety of factors can affect the color of dentine, including sunlight, acidity, and changes in temperature or humidity. While ivory and dentine are understood to be synonymous, craftspeople regularly incorporated cementum and material from the the cementum-dentine junction into their carvings. As a result, ivory objects will often have regions of different colors, which can become more pronounced in the burial environment (Figure 11). Additionally, subjecting ivory to excess temperatures can alter the color of the material. Ivory exposed to heat can take on shades ranging from bluish gray to black. As a result, color does not provide a reliable metric for determining whether an object is made from ivory, although it may be beneficial for differentiating different tissues within the tooth (e.g., enamel, dentine, and cementum).

3.3 The Pulp Cavity

The pulp cavity is a structure within teeth containing pulp, a collection of nerves, connective tissue, blood vessels, and specialized cells (odontoblasts)

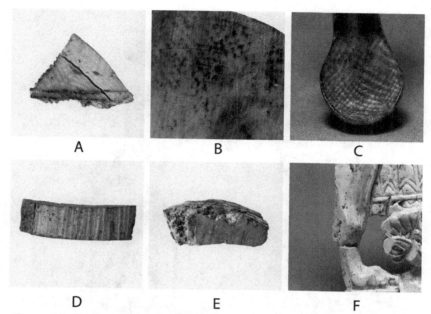

Figure 11 (A) Ivory fragment showing a transverse cut with a thick layer of cementum. Schreger pattern is faint closest to the cementum layer. (B) Detail view of the Schreger pattern presenting as a "checkerboard." (C) Detail view of the Schreger pattern. (D) A longitudinal surface of delaminated ivory (the "ghosts" of lamellae). (E) Transverse view of degraded ivory showing faint lines of lamellar growth (F) Detail of ivory carving showing longitudinal surface of delaminated ivory (the "ghosts" of lamellae).

Source: A, B, D, E: Photos by Jeff Vanderpool. Photos courtesy of the Ephoreia of Antiquities of Pieria and UCLA. C: Detail of an ivory spoon from Central Africa (late 1800s–early 1900s) from the Cleveland Museum of Art, accession number 2010.449. F: Detail of Levantine ivory carving from the Cleveland Museum of Art, accession number: 1968.46.

responsible for generating dentine; this region is crucial for the health and maintenance of the tooth. In most of the teeth used for ivory, the pulp cavity is widest at the proximal end and tapers toward the distal end. The pulp cavity closes and transitions into a portion of the tooth that is entirely composed of dentine. However, the proportion of the tooth occupied by the pulp cavity depends on the age of the animal, as well as the species. The narwhal tusk has a pulp cavity that runs throughout the entirety of the tooth, whereas the pulp cavity of an elephant tusk only occupies the first third of the tooth. For an ivory carver, the pulp cavity represents a hollow region that must be incorporated into the object or avoided altogether (Figure 12). Starting in the Bronze Age, and continuing until the medieval period, ivory carvers took advantage of the pulp cavity of proboscidean tusks to create pyxides.

Figure 12 Medieval statue (North French, ca. 1250 CE) of Mary and Jesus
made from elephant ivory that incorporates the pulp cavity.

Source: Metropolitan Museum of Art, accession number: 17.190.181a, b

3.4 Enamel

Enamel is a hard, mineralized tissue that acts as a protective outer layer on the
teeth of many species. Unlike other tissues, enamel is almost entirely inorganic,
with less than 1 percent organic material. Enamel has a shiny appearance and
is harder than both dentine and cementum; it often preserves better than other
dental tissues and skeletal materials like bone and antler. Walrus and elephant
tusks exhibit only small amounts of enamel which abrades away during the
course of the animal's life. As a result, most ivory carvings do not feature any
enamel. While enamel is not carved in the same manner as dentine, the material
still features within certain worked animal objects. For example, animal tooth
pendants often showcase an unmodified enamel surface. Additionally, craftspeople may incise enamel or cut sections of the tooth to highlight the enamel
surface (See Section 3.6).

3.5 Proboscidean Ivory

Proboscidean ivory represents the material made from the tusks (incisors)
of living elephant species (*Loxodonta cyclotis*, *Loxodonta africana*, *Elephas*

maximus) and their extinct relatives (e.g., *Palaeoloxodon sp.*, *Mammuthus sp.*, *Mammut sp.*, *Elephas sp.*, *and Stegodon sp.*). Two species of elephant remain extant in Africa: The African bush elephant (*Loxodonta africana*) and the African forest elephant (*Loxodonta cyclotis*). Males and females of both species develop tusks, but the tusks of females are generally smaller. The Asian elephant (*Elephas maximus*) has are three recognized subspecies: the Sri Lankan elephant (*Elephas maximus maximus*), the Indian elephant (*Elephas maximus indicus*), and the Sumatran elephant (*Elephas maximus sumatranus*). Among Asian elephants, only males develop proper tusks, whereas females can develop much smaller incisors known as tushes. The tusks of African bush elephants are the largest, while Asian elephants and African forest elephants have similarly sized tusks. While the ivory of living and extinct species can be potentially differentiated using the Schreger pattern and other scientific approaches, all proboscidean ivory is remarkably similar in its properties, structure, and appearance. As a result, identifying sources of ivory based on archaeological specimens or carved objects can be difficult, if not impossible, without destructive analysis.

Proboscidean ivory carving has a long history and a wide geographic distribution. In the Paleolithic period, mammoth ivory was an important material for the creation of tools and served as a medium for artistic representation. Several notable Paleolithic carvings were created with proboscidean ivory, including the Venus of Brassempouy, The Venus of Hohle Fells, and the Lion-man of Hohlenstein-Stadel. Proboscidean ivory continued to be used throughout the Neolithic and Chalcolithic periods in Europe and Asia, with impressive objects made from Asian and African elephant ivory made in Iberia between 3200 and 2300 BCE (Lucianez-Trivino et al. 2022). By the Late Bronze Age, ivory carving was widespread throughout the Levant, Mediterranean, Near East, and Northern Africa; it was found alongside other trade commodities on the Uluburun Shipwreck (coast of Turkey, late fourteenth century BCE). In central Asia, there is evidence for the production of ivory objects using the tusks of Asian elephants at the Oxus Civilization site of Gonur Depe (ca. 2400–1600 BCE, Turkmenistan) (Frenez 2018). Elsewhere in Asia, craftspeople in Shang Dynasty China produced ivory cups inlaid with turquoise, such as the one found at the Fuhao Tomb in Anyang (Shen 2002, 46).

By the first millennium BCE, elephant ivory became even more widely traded and produced. Craftspeople in the Mediterranean were responsible for large quantities of ivory objects used in elite contexts, most notably the Levantine ivory objects that were plundered by Assyria and later discovered at sites like Nimrud (Herrmann 2017). During the Classical period, elephant ivory was used in new ways, as craftspeople discovered how to "unscroll" it to create veneers for larger-than-life-sized Chryselephantine (gold and ivory) statuary; using ivory as a medium for large statuary continued into the Roman period as well (Lapatin 2001). During the first century CE, Southeast Asia emerged as a major center for the creation of ivory objects, with some of the best examples of this craft being the Begram ivories (found in eastern Afghanistan). During this period, ivories from this region were traded over great distances, as evidenced by the "Pompeii Lakshmi," an Indian carving found in the ruins of Pompeii (Mehendale 2001).

Between the eighth and fifteenth centuries CE, elephant ivory was a crucial material for the creation of liturgical and devotional Christian objects in Europe, used for a range of objects including sculpture and altarpieces. During roughly the same period (ninth century CE), another major tradition of ivory carving emerged in Islamic Iberia; craftspeople produced intricate carvings for the Umayyad court, including the Pyxis of al-Mughira and the Pyxis of Zamora (Makariou 2010). In many of these traditions of ivory carving, Africa served as the main source for the material. During the sixteenth century CE, clusters of ivory production formed across the western and central regions of the continent. (Afonso et al. 2022, 10). Both trade and looting by colonial powers brought many of these objects out of Africa, including the notable Benin ivory masks. One of the most recent major carving practices making use of ivory developed in Japan during the seventeenth century CE: Craftspeople used elephant ivory (among other materials) to create *netsuke*, objects initially used to fasten the cords around a container for holding objects, but later became luxury items.

3.5.1 Cementum

Unlike in the teeth of other species, cementum covers nearly the entirety of the outside of proboscidean tusks. The material is thickest at the proximal end, but present throughout the tusk. Cementum exhibits ridges that run parallel to the length of the tusk (Figure 13A), although the ridges can also appear less pronounced (Figure 13B). Unlike dentine, cementum lacks indications of concentric growth and is not made up of dentinal tubules, so diagnostic patterns like the Lines of Owen or Schreger lines are absent. It can, however, become delaminated from the dentine at the Cementum-Dentine Junction. Within the context of proboscidean ivory carving, cementum has been referred to as "bark," and sometimes carvers removed the material (Stern 2007, 27). However, there are many examples of finished ivory objects that retain regions of cementum. As it was more likely to be discarded, the presence of cementum (or pieces of ivory retaining cementum) in an archaeological context may be an indication of an ivory production space.

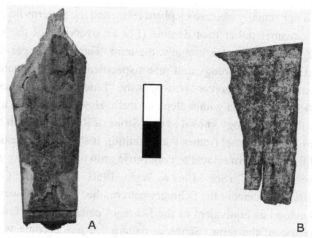

Figure 13 Ivory production waste from ancient Methone (ca. 700 BCE). (A):
Cementum of an elephant tusk showing cut marks; (B): degraded piece of
cementum of an elephant tusk showing cut marks.
Source: Photographs by Jeff Vanderpool.

3.5.2 Dentine

The dentine of proboscidean tusks is found underneath the outer layer of
cementum. It occupies most of the incisor and follows the same curved shape
of the tusk. As in the teeth of other species, the pulp cavity occupies roughly the
first third of the tusk (the proximal region). The pulp cavity exhibits a similar
shape to the tusk itself: a conical region tapering toward the distal end. While
ivory carvers needed to be conscientious of the hollow region of the tusk, the
amount of dentine within the distal portion of larger tusks could have provided
craftspeople enough material to create works which do not incorporate the pulp
cavity. Additionally, craftspeople could remove rectangular sections of ivory
from around the pulp cavity as well. As a result, plaques and smaller sculp-
tural works will not necessarily show any sign of the pulp cavity. Owing to
the incremental growth processes of proboscidean dentine, there are a series of
diagnostic features that can help identify the material.

3.5.3 Schreger Pattern

One of the most distinct characteristics of ivory is a series of light and dark
regions present on transverse sections of the tusk. Scholars have associated
multiple scientists with the discovery of this pattern (including Schreger, Retzius, and Owen), which has led to some confusion about its name. This pattern
is most often described as "Schreger lines" or "Schreger pattern" even though

Schreger did not actually observe elephant teeth, and the patterns he described were within enamel rather than dentine (For an overview of the term, see Espinoza & Mann 1993). Additionally, the term "Hunter-Schreger Bands" is widely used in dental histology and refers specifically to the enamel bands. Some scholars describe this ivory pattern as the "Lines of Retzius," as Retzius described the phenomenon within elephant teeth. However, there is a separate term within dental histology known as the "Striae of Retzius," which describes growth lines within enamel (rather than dentine). It should also be noted that there is a different pattern related to concentric growth within ivory described as the "Lines of Owen" (See Miles & White 1960, 778). While Owen was one of the first to document the Schreger pattern, the "Lines of Owen" should not be understood as equivalent to the Schreger pattern. While few initially adopted the use of the term "Schreger pattern," it has become widespread among scholars and non-scholars alike. As a result, this work acknowledges the contributions of the other researchers (e.g., Retzius and Owen), but will continue to use the term "Schreger pattern" for clarity.

The Schreger pattern often appears as a series of interconnected V-shaped bands known as Schreger or "engine-turned" lines. As this pattern is unique to proboscideans, it is considered one of the best metrics for characterizing ivory. When illustrating Schreger lines, most guides will provide an image of a cross section of modern tusk. Such images clearly display the pattern, but they are not always helpful for identifying archaeological materials. As worked ivory objects were carved from a variety of orientations within the tusk, the transverse surface may not be evident on every archaeological specimen. Additionally, the Schreger pattern is less pronounced in certain areas of the tusk, including the regions nearer to the cementum-dentine junction and the region closest to center of the tusk (Figure 11A). Even if the archaeological object captures a transverse section of ivory where the Schreger pattern should be visible, the preservation environment has a marked effect on the coloration of the surface and appearance of the pattern. As a result, the Schreger pattern may appear as the typical series of pronounced V-shaped lines, faint lines, or even as a checkerboard (Figure 11A–C). While the Schreger pattern is one of the best criteria for establishing whether an object is made from proboscidean ivory, both the preservation and orientation of the carving can affect whether it is present.

The Schreger pattern also offers a quantitative basis for determining the species of proboscidean to which the ivory belongs. A series of studies have demonstrated that different proboscidean species have distinct ranges of angles of intersecting Schreger lines. Ivory from mammoth species exhibits acute Schreger angles ($< 90°$), whereas extant species tend to show larger angles. Additionally, the Schreger angles of Asian elephants appear consistently smaller than those of African elephants. The outer Schreger angles, those located nearer to the cementum, are larger than those closer to the center of the tusk (inner Schreger lines). Additionally, Schreger angles can vary depending on whether they are recorded closer to the proximal or distal end of the tusk. Moreover, many of the studies of Schreger angles have been conducted using large portions of ivory cut to a precise transverse section, allowing researchers to control for these variables. As a result, archaeological samples of ivory are not likely to give enough information to make an accurate determination about species.

3.5.4 Lamellae and Cone-within-Cone Splitting

The incremental layers of growth (lamellae) within proboscidean dentine are often visible to the naked eye and can be used to distinguish ivory from other materials (Figure 11E). However, detecting lamellae can often depend on both the condition of the ivory and the original orientation of the object within the tusk. The lamellae grow in increments, often giving dentine a banded appearance. This pattern, known as the "lines of Owen," often co-occurs with a different diagnostic feature of ivory called "cone-within-cone splitting." Cone-within-cone splitting is an effect of the tusk becoming delaminated around its regions of concentric growth, resulting in a series of regular cracks that run through the material. As this feature is thought to result from changes in humidity, cone-within-cone splitting may be more likely to occur in archaeological specimens than in more modern objects. Other animal materials may be prone to cracking, but cone-within-cone splitting has a shape and regularity that differentiates it from similar effects of deposition in other materials.

Within a transverse cross section of a tusk, cone-within-cone splitting will present as a series of circular cracks which radiate from the center, whereas a longitudinal cut shows cone-within-cone splitting as a parabolic set of cracks (Figure 14). As objects are not always carved from a portion of the tusk that is parallel to the longitudinal or transverse axis, cone-within-cone splitting may also appear as a series of elliptical lines. However, many ivory objects are carved so that their original orientation within the tusk is not immediately obvious, and cone-within-cone splitting will not necessarily occur throughout the entire object; detecting cone-within-cone splitting requires identifying multiple parallel cracks (Figure 15).

The longitudinal surfaces of delaminated ivory have a ridged appearance which Krzyszkowska (1990, 90) refers to as the "ghosts" of lamellae (Figure 11 D and F). This feature is common in archaeological examples of proboscidean ivory due to cone-within-cone splitting, although hippopotamus ivory can also

Figure 14 Back of a Levantine horse frontlet carved from longitudinal section of the elephant tusk showing parabolic cone-within-cone splitting (ca. ninth–eighth centuries BCE).

Source: Metropolitan Museum of Art, accession number: 61.197.5.

Figure 15 Levantine ivory carving showing deterioration typical of cone-within-cone splitting (ca. ninth–eighth centuries BCE). The right image shows highlighted sections of cone-within-cone splitting.

Source: Cleveland Museum of Art, accession number: 1968.46.

exhibit the same patterns (Banerjee et al. 2017). As a result, the "ghosts" of lamellae should not be seen as a diagnostic trait of proboscidean ivory, but they can be used to distinguish ivory from bone or antler.

3.6 Suid Ivory

Several species and subspecies of suids, including warthogs (*Phacochoerus africanus*, *Phacochoerus aethiopicus*), wild boar (*Sus scrofa* and its many subspecies), and domestic pig (*Sus scrofa domesticus*), develop sizable canine teeth that were modified by people in the past. Male suids develop canines that are larger and morphologically different from the teeth of females, making them the more desirable material for craftspeople. The lower canines of males provide the most material, although upper canines were occasionally carved as well. Like the teeth of other animals, suid canines exhibit a pulp cavity that tapers toward the distal end. The proximal end of the canine appears mostly hollow, while the center and distal end have significantly more dentine. The distal end of suid canines exhibits a flat surface resulting from the teeth cutting into one another. This wear facet can resemble an anthropogenically modified surface, but it is a natural feature of the tooth. While the canine teeth of wild and domestic pigs share many similarities with those of warthogs, there are morphological differences that can be used to tell these two materials apart.

3.6.1 Pig and Boar

The lower canines of pigs and boars can most easily be distinguished by their distinct shape: a trihedral/triangular cross section. Two of the sides of the canine are covered in a thin layer of enamel, while the remaining side exhibits exposed dentine. The dentine exhibits a more uniform surface in both color and texture, while the enamel appears glossy, with a series of lunate ridges that occur in the transverse direction (perpendicular to the length of the tooth). Like the canine teeth of hippopotami, pig and boar canines possess a V-shaped interstitial zone that is visible in a transverse section.

On lower canines, the wear facet tends to be small and narrow, making up only a small portion of the total length of the tooth. Upper canines are slightly more curved than lower canines and have a bulbous rounded shape in cross section. The upper canines are likewise only partially covered in enamel, with a section of exposed dentine. The wear facet is significantly longer and wider, taking up a considerable portion of the length of the tooth. As so much dentine is exposed, the darker interstitial zone can often be seen as a black line running parallel to the length of the tooth within this region. Compared to other forms of ivory, the dentine of pigs and boars appears dense and homogeneous with only faint signs of growth lines (not always visible and best viewed with a flashlight).

People in the past approached suid canines in different ways; craftspeople often used these teeth as pendants, with little modification beyond a drill hole or attachment. However, Japanese *netsuke* carvers created designs in relief on the surface of suid teeth, often preserving the overall shape of the material. In a wholly different approach to the material, the Mycenaean Greeks used the canines of boars to create helmet plates. Rather than carve the dentine of the tooth, Mycenaean craftspeople created flat sections from the enamel while cutting most of the dentine away. In a strict sense, the enamel plaques cannot be called boar ivory, as most of the dentine was removed.

3.6.2 Warthog (Phacochoerus sp.)

Warthog canines are significantly larger than the canines of pigs and boars and can be as large as the teeth of hippopotami. In addition to differences in size, the canine teeth of warthogs are distinguishable from those of pigs and boars based on several morphological features. Owing to two longitudinal grooves that run the length of the tooth, the canine teeth of warthogs appear "waisted" or "pinched" at the center; the overall shape is also markedly rectangular (see Baker et al. 2020, 51 and Figure 16). Unlike the homogeneous dentine within the canines of pigs and boars, the dentine of warthog canines exhibits visible growth lines. These dentinal layers surround a conspicuous interstitial zone that is straight, as opposed to the V-shaped interstitial zone that typifies the canines of pigs, boars, and hippopotami.

3.7 Hippopotamus Ivory

Hippopotamus ivory is derived from the dentine from the canines and incisors of the animal. The hippopotamus has two upper canines and two lower canines

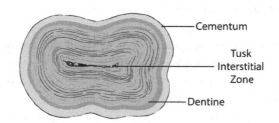

Canine

Figure 16 Drawing of a warthog canine tooth in cross section.
Source: Drawing by Leah Olson.

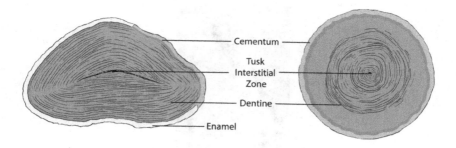

Lower Canine   Incisor

Figure 17 Drawing of a hippopotamus canine and incisor in cross section.
Source: Drawing by Leah Olson.

which are markedly larger. While the shapes of the teeth do not vary between males and females, there can be considerable differences in size. As the canines are continuously growing, the upper and lower teeth come in contact, creating a wear facet on the surface of the teeth; both the upper and lower canines are curved and roughly triangular in cross section. The upper canine tends to appear slightly rounded or heart-shaped, while the lower canine is more angular (Figure 17). Hippopotamus canines are mostly by enamel on two sides, with a third section of exposed cementum (similar to *suid* teeth, Hillson 2005, 132). While the exposed cementum is smooth, the enamel is composed of defined ridges that extend the length of the tooth. Craftspeople are likely to have removed the enamel before carving the dentine, although Krzyszkowska (1988, 214) points out that "the hardness of the enamel, comparable to jade or agate, presents a greater obstacle to carvers than the 'bark' of elephant tusk." Hippopotami typically exhibit four upper and lower incisors, which are straight and pointed. Often described as "peg shaped," the incisors of hippopotami are round in cross section (Figure 17). The lower incisors are fully coated in enamel, whereas the upper incisors "just have an enamel stripe" (Hillson 2005, 132). Unlike the canines, the incisors do not develop facets from contact with other teeth, although they tend to wear to a point through use.

As in the teeth of other animals, the canines and incisors contain a pulp cavity that starts at the proximal end of the tooth and tapers toward the distal end. Within the lower canines, the pulp cavity gives way to the commissure, a region where the inner dentine (i.e., the newest dentine) is formed. This region is equivalent to the interstitial zone and appears as a slightly curved line in the center of the tusk within a transverse section. It is markedly different from the rest of the tooth, with a grayish color and heterogeneous composition (Figure 18). In a transverse section, the lamellae encircle this region as a series of wavy bands, mirroring the triangular shape of the tooth.

Figure 18 Fragment of an Egyptian clapper from the Middle Kingdom
(ca. 1900–1640 BCE) showing inner dentine, outer dentine, and commissure
of hippopotamus ivory.

Source: Metropolitan Museum of Art, accession number: 22.1.105.

Within a longitudinal section of the canine, the regions of inner and outer
dentine appear different from one another (see Figure 19). Unlike in a transverse section, the lines of the lamellae do not have an orderly orientation.
Instead, they appear wavy, with some of the lines creating more circular or
curved patterns. The inner dentine presents as a narrow band that extends out-
ward from the pulp cavity. The inner and outer dentine are separated from one
another by a fine line that is punctuated by darker areas that present as small
dots (< 1 mm). This dividing line corresponds to the commissure viewed in
a transverse section. Moreover, the texture and color of the inner and outer
dentine may differ from one another. The commissure is visible within only
a portion of the tusk, so it is possible for craftspeople to create objects from
the outer dentine alone. As a result, many diagnostic aspects of hippopotamus
ivory may be absent from finished objects.

Within the inner dentine, the lamellae present as a set of wavy lines that reach
a slight peak in the center of the commissure. The lamellae of the outer dentine are noticeably different, appearing smaller, closer together, more evenly

Figure 19 Fragment of an Egyptian magic wand from the Middle Kingdom (ca. 1900–1802 BCE) showing outer dentine of hippopotamus ivory.
Source: Metropolitan Museum of Art, accession number: 22.1.105.

spaced, and running parallel to the length of the tooth. The overall appearance of the commissure viewed in a longitudinal section is akin to the shape of a curved hourglass. Krzyszkowska reports that the commissure is a naturally weak point "from which arises a natural line of fracture," providing several illustrations showing a lengthwise break through the canine. It should be noted that this fracture is not present on all hippopotamus canines, but it might be more likely to be observed on archaeological specimens.

The incisors do not exhibit markedly different layers of inner and outer dentine. The appearance of the dentine shows fine growth lines which follow the circular structure of the tooth. Closest to the center of the tooth, the dentine may appear slightly darker than in outer layers. While the incisor does not exhibit a pronounced interstitial zone, it shows a small dark spot (called the "heartline" by Krzyszkowska) in the center that runs nearly the entire length of the tooth.

3.8 Walrus Ivory

Walrus ivory comes from the large upper incisors that characterize the species. In a transverse section, the shape of the walrus incisor is between a rectangle and ellipse and three dental tissues can be clearly differentiated from one another: a cementum layer, followed by primary dentine, and a core of secondary dentine (Figure 20). At the proximal end of the tusk, the outer layer of cementum is thicker and more pronounced. The cementum often appears whiter than the primary and secondary dentine in fresh or well-preserved tusks, while

Figure 20 Transverse section of walrus ivory.

Source: Microscopy and imaging by Tim Bromage and members of the Bromage lab.

the dentine is more yellow. As with other animal materials, the coloration is highly dependent on the state of preservation.

The primary dentine is dense with fine growth layers that radiate from the center and follow the shape of the tooth. The most diagnostic aspect of walrus ivory is the secondary dentine, which is often described as appearing "oatmeal-like." The secondary dentine is composed of many circular regions known as "denticles" that form within the dentine. Depending on the preservation, this region of secondary dentine may not look as white as the outer dentine and may appear more translucent. Owing to the nature of the inner dentine, this area may also be more prone to preservation issues. This can be seen among

Figure 21 Detail of a medieval walrus ivory carving showing the "oatmeal" of the secondary dentine. British or North French (1000–1050 CE).
Source: Metropolitan Museum of Art, accession number: 17.190.217

certain pieces of the "Lewis Chessmen," which exhibit hollow sections owing to the loss of secondary dentine. Moreover, Hillson (2005, 189) reports that the denticles can come loose within teeth specimens and "rattle about on shaking."

Observing the differences between the primary and secondary dentine is the best way of identifying walrus ivory. The secondary dentine occupies a large portion of the center of the tusk, meaning that it was often an unavoidable aspect of the material for ivory carvers. A view of the top of a medieval walrus ivory pectoral (component of a large cross) shows a clear delineation between the primary and secondary layers (Figure 21). Likewise, another medieval ivory plaque was almost entirely carved within the secondary ivory (Figure 22). Because these types of dentine are so different from one another, certain groups of craftspeople may have tried to carve exclusively within the more homogeneous primary dentine (LeMoine & Darwent 1998, 79).

3.9 Narwhal Ivory

Narwhals have a series of small teeth at the upper jaw, one of which forms into a long, spiral-shaped tusk that grows up to 3 meters. The length and spiral shape are the most distinct features of this tooth. Unlike the teeth of other species, the narwhal tusk has a pulp cavity that runs throughout the entirety of the tusk. Craftspeople must account for the hollow portion of the tooth, a quality that makes narwhal tusk more prone to breakage. The outer surface of the narwhal tusk lacks enamel and is covered in a thick layer of cementum. Figure 23 shows a transverse view taken from a thin section of a narwhal tusk. The image was captured in artificially high contrast, accentuating the

Figure 22 Ivory scene carved primarily within the "oatmeal" of the secondary dentine. Germany, Lower Rhine Valley, Romanesque period (1050–1100 CE).

Source: Cleveland Museum of Art, accession number: 1922.359

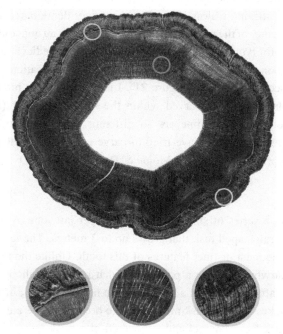

Figure 23 Transverse Section of Narwhal Ivory.

Source: Microscopy and imaging by Tim Bromage and members of the Bromage lab.

differences between the cementum and the dentine. In this view, the cementum-dentine junction is thick and clearly distinguishable. Moreover, the cementum, dentine, and cementum-dentine junction tend to vary in color, resulting in a series of clear layers between the outer and inner regions of the tusk; however, all of these materials are prone to color change in archaeological environments.

Craftspeople often chose to preserve the spiral surface of the narwhal tusk, resulting in finished objects that retain the outer cementum layer of the tooth (e.g., decorative plates of sword hilts and drinking cups). Owing to the recognizable shape of the tusk, the material used in such objects is easily distinguishable as narwhal tusk. However, craftspeople also treated the tusk like other sources of ivory: carving the actual dentine, removing the cementum, and incorporating or excluding the pulp cavity from the finished product. As a result, observing aspects of the dentine itself may be critical for recognizing narwhal ivory.

3.10 Ivory from Other Marine Mammals

The teeth of cetaceans, the infraorder of marine mammals that includes whales, dolphins, and porpoises, have been exploited for their ivory across multiple continents for thousands of years. Cetacean ivory comes from several species of the suborder *Odontoceti*, also known as toothed whales; the category of toothed whales encompasses several cetacean species including dolphins and orcas. In contrast to baleen whales (suborder *Mysticeti*) that rely on filter feeding and have only small vestigial teeth, toothed whales have rows of conical teeth that are similar in appearance. Owing to their large teeth and wide habitat, the sperm whale (*Physeter macrocephalus*) has been used as a source of ivory more often than other marine mammals. There is also some archaeological evidence for the use of teeth from other odontocetes: An example of a modified orca (*Orcinus orca*) tooth was found at a Late Norse site in Scotland. That same site also produced examples of unmodified teeth from small delphinoids and teeth from a beaked whale (Evans 2021, 210–211). Unmodified orca teeth have also been found at a site inhabited by indigenous populations of the Pacific Northwest of America (Huelsbeck 1988, 4).

Due to their homogeneity, whale teeth are not classified in the same way (e.g., incisor, canine, and molar) as the teeth of other mammals. Like other mammals, whales have a tapering pulp cavity that occupies the first (proximal) third of their teeth. The teeth of sperm whales are covered in a relatively thick layer of cementum, with a small tip of enamel (Figure 24). As the animal ages, the teeth become worn and may be reduced in size (Hillson 2005, 69). The teeth of whales are highly diagnostic in a longitudinal section, which

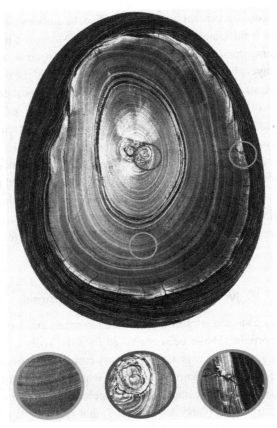

Figure 24 Transverse Section of Sperm Whale ivory.
Source: Microscopy and imaging by Tim Bromage and members of the Bromage lab.

clearly shows the boundary between the cementum and the dentine; the cementum layer appears thickest at the center of the tooth. In longitudinal section, the majority of the tooth is occupied by dentinal layers that appear as V-shaped annual growth lines oriented at roughly the same angle as the pulp cavity. In a transverse section, the growth lines are visible as elliptical bands that encircle the center of the tooth; the cementum-dentine junction is clearly defined as a gray band, usually darker than both the cementum and the dentine. Figure 24 shows a transverse section of a sperm whale tooth in high contrast to accentuate the differences between the layers. The teeth of orcas are like those of sperm whales: Both exhibit visible lamellar layers in a transverse section. However, the cementum layer in orca teeth is markedly thinner, making it easy to distinguish between the two taxa if the cementum layer is present (Baker et al. 2020, 35). Some of the most common forms of modified whale teeth come from scrimshanders (individuals who practice the craft of scrimshaw) in the Atlantic Ocean. While this artistic tradition encompasses a range of materials (e.g., whale bone, baleen, and shell) and techniques, many examples of scrimshaw were created by incising lines into the cementum of the teeth of whales. These techniques do not actually alter the shape of the tooth, meaning that the material often remains identifiable.

In addition to the objects made from cetacean teeth, the incisors of dugongids have also served as a source of ivory. Dugongids are a family (*Dugongidae*) in the order of Sirenia comprising the marine sea cow (*Dugong dugon*) and the extinct Steller's sea cow (*Hydrodamalis gigas*). Sirenia are closely related to proboscideans and dugongids also produce continuously growing upper incisors that resemble tusks. Like in proboscideans, dugongid incisors are composed primarily of dentine, which is covered by an external layer of cementum. Additionally, the incisors have a single section of enamel on one surface of the tooth (Hillson 2005, 120). Both male and female dugongids produce incisors, which Nganvongpanit et al. (2017) were able to distinguish based on the pulp cavity: Incisors belonging to male dugongids generally have larger pulp cavities and incisors belonging to females were almost entirely made up of dentine. Dugongid incisors do not necessarily have the same curvature as an elephant or walrus tusk. Instead, dugongid incisors can exhibit an appearance that is more angular or L-shaped, which is sometimes preserved in the shape of worked objects.

Archaeological examples of objects made from dugongid incisors were found at a Neolithic site on the Arab Peninsula (Uerpmann et al. 2012), as well as at a site in the Solomon Islands dating to 1500 CE (Leach et al. 1979). Additionally, more contemporary (non-archaeological) examples of dugongid ivory objects are still being traded in Southeast Asia (Lee & Nijman 2015), suggesting that this material was carved in a wide range of areas adjacent to dugongid habitats.

3.11 Non-ivory Teeth

Certain objects made from teeth found in archaeological assemblages were modified, but not for the purpose of carving dentine. Evidence for the creation of pendants made from teeth predates the Holocene period and has a wide geographic distribution. Craftspeople often chose the canine teeth of predators or wild animals as recognizable symbols of the animals that provided the material; such pendants could be made from canids (dogs/wolves), bears, suids (boars/pigs), or other animals. Craftspeople also chose less conspicuous teeth, including the vestigial upper canines of different species of elk (e.g., *Cervus canadensis* and *Alces alces*). Sometimes referred to as "elk ivory," the dentine itself was rarely modified (Mannermaa et al. 2020). Additionally, there is evidence for the use of shark teeth in a similar manner. Archaeological examples of shark teeth have been found at many sites in the Americas, with a smaller subset showing evidence of modification (Betts et al. 2012, 637–640). Creating such pendants usually represents only a minimal modification (e.g., a drill hole or cut groove) of the tooth, such that it remains identifiable.

3.12 Differentiating Ivory from Bone and Antler

While there are several criteria for identifying ivory from other skeletal tissue, proper identification is contingent on an understanding of the structure of these materials. The ability to hypothesize the position of the worked object within the original organic structure makes it easier to evaluate whether the object in question fulfills the criteria that characterize a given material. The spongy, open appearance of trabecular structures in bone, antler, and horn core are unique to these materials and do not form in dentine. As a result, observations of trabecular material can be used to rule out ivory definitively. While trabecular tissue is easily distinguished, the cortical portions of bone and antler can appear similar to ivory. These materials often exhibit a slightly porous structure that is a result of the canal systems that bring nutrients to the bone (see Section 2). The parts of the canal systems nearest to the surface tend to appear slightly darker because the hollow structures become discolored or are in shadow, although the appearance of the canal systems differs depending on how the bone object was oriented when it was modified. Worked surfaces that are abraded or cut along the length of a long bone can expose the Haversian canals, appearing as small cracks oriented along the length of the object. In cases where the bone has been cut closer to the transverse axis, Haversian canals will appear more like circular points. In either case, the structure of cortical bone has an irregular, grainy appearance that is markedly different from ivory. Ivory tends to look less porous and more homogeneous, often described as having a "dense" appearance.

The morphology of teeth is complex, composed of multiple layers of tissue (e.g., enamel, cementum, and dentine). When more than one of these layers is visible, they can be highly diagnostic (see Tables 2 and 3). Moreover, the qualities of the dentine itself like lamellar growth layers can provide clear features that distinguish it from bone. Other dentine-specific attributes may further characterize the ivory (e.g., denticles in walrus ivory and Schreger pattern in proboscidean ivory), giving an indication of the taxa (see Table 4).

Overall Shape: Does the shape of the material conform to any recognizable skeletal morphological features (e.g., the presence of hollow interior section that may correspond to the medullary cavity)? Alternatively, is there a tapering cavity that may correspond to a pulp cavity?

Appearance: Evidence of trabeculae or osteonic canals are strong indications that an object is made from bone. Alternatively, indications of growth layers point to dentine.

Pitfalls and Possible Misidentifications: Small sections of cortical bone that are polished can exhibit a uniform appearance that may be mistaken for dentine. Dentine that is cut in certain orientations may not show clear evidence for lamellae or other diagnostic features; the inability to recognize a diagnostic feature in ivory is not necessarily evidence that the material is bone or antler. Moreover, it is possible for bone to fracture in ways that imitate cone-within-cone splitting.

Table 2 Shape of tooth and layers within

Tooth	Transverse section	Layers
Proboscidean incisor	Elliptical	Enamel (at tips, often abraded away), Cementum, Dentine
Suid canine (Boar/Pig)	Trihedral	Enamel (on two sides), Cementum, Dentine
Suid canine (Warthog)	Elliptical-rectangular	Cementum, Dentine
Hippopotamus canine	Trihedral	Enamel (two sides), Cementum, Dentine
Hippopotamus incisor	Elliptical-circular	Enamel (only partially on the upper incisors), Cementum, Dentine
Walrus incisor	Elliptical	Cementum, Primary dentine, Secondary dentine
Narwhal incisor	Spiral exterior	Cementum, Dentine
Sperm whale tooth	Elliptical	Cementum, Dentine
Orca tooth	Nearly rectangular	Cementum, Dentine

Table 3 Appearance of cementum

Tooth	Appearance of cementum
Proboscidean incisor	Similar in appearance to the dentine, lacks the Schreger pattern
Suid canine (Boar/Pig)	Cementum covers only the inner-facing side of the tooth, and the other two sides are covered by enamel.
Suid canine (Warthog)	Relatively thick band of cementum, which is usually a lighter color than the dentine.
Hippopotamus canine	One of the trihedral sides is covered in cementum, while the other two are covered in enamel.
Hippopotamus incisor	Thin band of cementum.
Walrus incisor	Relatively thick band of cementum, with a distinct white color at the cementum-dentine junction.
Narwhal incisor	Markedly thick and different in color than both the cementum-dentine junction and the dentine. The cementum-dentine junction appears as the lightest part of the cross section.
Sperm whale tooth	Thick and normally different color than the dentine. The border between cementum and dentine presents as a dark line.
Orca tooth	Thin layer of cementum with a cementum-dentine junction that appears lighter than the surrounding cementum and dentine.

4 Keratinous Materials

Keratin is a fibrous protein that makes up a range of structures within animal bodies, including hair, nails, claws, hooves, scales, and horns. Like other animal materials, keratinous tissues were used for the creation of objects across different cultures and time periods. Owing to its low mineral content, as well as the exposure of the protein to chemical and microbial attack, keratin is particularly susceptible to decay and rarely found in archaeological contexts outside of highly arid, frozen, or anaerobic burial environments (O'Connor et al. 2015, 395). As a result, evidence for the creation and use of keratinous objects is often difficult to detect directly within the archaeological record. When keratinous objects are preserved, precise identification can be challenging.

Table 4 Appearance of dentine

Tooth	Appearance of the dentine
Proboscidean incisor	Distinct Schreger pattern, tendency toward "cone-within-cone" splitting
Suid canine (Boar/Pig)	Dense, opaque, relatively non-descript
Suid canine (Warthog)	Fine growth lines that are in the same shape as the transverse section. The center of the tusk has a linear interstitial zone.
Hippopotamus canine	Interstitial zone appears as an arched line in the center, with fine concentric growth lines radiating from the center and following the trihedral shape
Hippopotamus incisor	Homogeneous, with fine growth lines visible at the center of the tusk (interstitial zone).
Walrus incisor	Primary dentine: Homegenous. Secondary dentine: Crystalline, semi-translucent, spherical.
Narwhal incisor	Fine concentric growth lines.
Sperm whale tooth	Fine concentric growth lines.
Orca tooth	Fine concentric growth lines.

Keratinous materials are incredibly malleable and versatile, allowing crafts-people to stretch and manipulate them into a variety of shapes and colors. While hard tissues like bone may exhibit specific morphological landmarks, craftspeople can wholly alter the shape of a keratinous material.

Kerantious materials exhibit a variety of visual characteristics: Horn can have different degrees of translucency and variegated color, baleen tends to exhibit a dark brown or black coloration that is semi-translucent, while tortoise-shell typically has a multicolored appearance. However, coloration and opacity are strongly dependent on the level of preservation. Archaeological examples of keratinous materials tend to lose translucency, appearing more like bone or other opaque organic materials. Most keratinous materials (e.g., horn, hoof, and baleen) possess a shared morphological composition: A series of tubules arranged in a linear structure, resulting in a highly striated appearance. When viewed perpendicular to their length, these tubules appear as a highly porous surface.

4.1 Horn and Horn Core

Horns are cranial appendages found among species of pronghorns and bovids (e.g., cattle, antelopes, sheep, and goats). Horns are more often found among male species, although females of many species also grow horns. An animal's horn is made up of a bony center known as the horn core and an outer keratinous layer, which is synonymous with the material known as horn. The horn core is mostly hollow, allowing the appendage to bend during the animal's life. Horn core is visually similar to the rest of the skeleton, but it is primarily composed of trabecular bone and it exhibits a porous surface owing to the smaller proportion of cortical bone. The exterior surface of horn core exhibits trabeculae which are markedly linear, showing long canal-like formations running parallel to the length of the appendage (Figure 25). Horn cores of cattle have an especially porous surface, while the exterior of sheep or goat horn core tends to be slightly smoother. Owing to the issues of keratin preservation, archaeologists might recover horn core in large quantities without ever discovering any traces of the horn itself.

Horn is one of the most common keratinous materials and has been employed by humans since as early as the Neolithic period (Lisowski 2014). Horn is often compared to plastic and is highly malleable. Craftspeople who use horn (sometimes known as horners) can work it into a variety of shapes, including knife hafts and combs. Horn can also be turned into a thin sheet, a technique used for window and lantern panes, as well as translucent covers for "hornbooks." It is

Figure 25 A worked piece of horn core of a sheep or goat showing a transverse cut from the site of ancient Methone (ca. 700 BCE).
Source: Photographs by Jeff Vanderpool.

an incredibly versatile material and may have been used in a variety of ways in the past, many of which are invisible in the archaeological record.

Horn develops as a series of sequential layers of growth like elephant ivory, giving it a similar cone-within-cone structure. This material often exhibits ridges perpendicular to the length of the appendage that marks layers of successive growth. O'Connor et al. (2015, 396–398) observe species-level visual and morphological features that help to distinguish the horn of different taxa. The authors note that sheep and goat horn generally lack pigmentation and is transparent, whereas the horn of buffalo and cattle can be pigmented and opaque.

4.2 Baleen

Baleen is the keratinous material that makes up the filter-feeding system found in the mouths of baleen whales (*Mysticeti*, e.g., blue whales, gray whales, and humpback whales). This structure is composed of a series of triangular sheets that have a fringe of fibrous bristles. Like other keratinous materials, baleen could be altered and molded to suit many uses, and craftspeople targeted it for its flexibility. It was used by Inuit, American, European, and Japanese cultures for a variety of purposes, including as a material in baskets, fishing line, collar stiffeners, bed webbing, tea trays, and shoehorns (Lauffenburger 1993, 220, see table 1). Since the 1600s, baleen has also been referred to as "whalebone" despite its keratinous composition. While "whalebone" is an inaccurate description of the material, the term is still occasionally used in publications and museum records.

The structure of baleen varies throughout the material. Baleen has a solid shell, often described as a "horn-like covering," that encloses a central layer of tubular structures that are visible to the naked eye. Hair-like bristles are present at the edge of the baleen plates, extending from regions where the horn-like covering has worn away (Figure 26). Objects made from baleen will not necessarily exhibit these diagnostic features, as craftspeople often split the material longitudinally to make use of the outer layers (O'Connor 1987, 19). Baleen objects tend to have a semi-translucent color that ranges from brownish amber to deep black, although coloration is highly dependent on the preservation conditions (in cases of archaeological examples). Objects made from baleen exhibit an even, linear composition that parallels the length of the triangular sheet and the direction of the central tubule layer. The bristles are wholly different, and owing to their structure, can be easily confused for mammalian hair (O'Connor 1987, 19). Like other keratinous materials, baleen is only found in

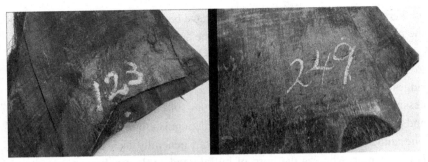

Figure 26 Details from a sheet of baleen showing the tubules.
Source: Smithsonian Museum, accession number: 2082996.

certain preservation environments. Archaeological examples of Baleen can be found in arctic environments (Mouël & Mouël 2002, 175; Sinding et al. 2012) and recovery of the material in temperate environments is far rarer; O'Connor and collaborators (2015, 394; 2017) highlight only a few instances of baleen found in the Netherlands (Bartels 2005, 59; Rijkelijkhuizen 2009, 414) and the United Kingdom (Moffat et al. 2008; O'Connor & O'Connor 2017).

4.3 Tortoiseshell

The shells of turtles are covered in keratinous scutes, which were used as a material by craftspeople in the past that is commonly referred to as "tortoiseshell." Tortoiseshell most often comes from the hawksbill sea turtle (*Eretmochelys imbricata*) and the green turtle (*Chelonia mydas*), although textual sources suggest that other species were used in the past (Casson 1989, 101–102). After being worked, the melanin within the tortoiseshell can take on a variety of colors, ranging from a pale yellow to shades of blue and green. Despite the mottled appearance, this material also exhibits a degree of transparency. Tortoiseshell was exploited throughout the world, with textual evidence for extensive trade throughout the Indian Ocean, as well as archaeological evidence for the material in the Americas (Frazier 2002, 12–18, 26–29; Frazier & Ishihara-Brito 2012). Like horn, tortoiseshell was modified using heat and used to create a wide variety of objects, including inlay, combs, pins, and fishhooks. Unlike horn and baleen, tortoiseshell does not have visible striations running through the material. The archaeological preservation of tortoiseshell is highly variable; O'Connor and collaborators (2015, 405) observe a delamination process that results in a separation of layers and a loss of transparency.

4.4 Differentiating Osseous and Keratinous Materials

Owing to differences in preservation environments, the appearance of archaeological keratinous materials can vary immensely.

The most decayed specimens of keratinous materials cannot be specifically identified without scientific analysis, although osseous and keratinous materials often appear sufficiently dissimilar to differentiate them from one another. However, the striations seen in keratinous materials could be mistaken for the lamellae of dentine, especially in cases where very little of the material remains.

FACTORS TO CONSIDER

General Appearance: Keratinous materials may have some degree of translucency, which is absent in bone and antler, and rare within materials derived from animal teeth. Keratinous materials exhibit very evident growth lines that are usually recognizable, even among modified objects.

Preservation and Context: Does the site have exceptional or unique preservation (e.g., high aridity or anaerobic conditions)? Alternatively, was the material under consideration found in a unique context (e.g., a grave) that could have contributed to its survival? Does it exhibit metal staining or was it contact with metal, which may also explain its continued preservation.

Pitfalls and Possible Misidentifications: The original shape of keratinous materials is rarely helpful for analyzing archaeological objects, as both craftspeople and subsequent taphonomic activities likely altered the structure of the material. The remains of the linear tubules within horn could be confused for the lamellae of ivory on a longitudinal surface (e.g., the so-called "ghosts"). Particularly degraded tortoiseshell can display delamination that could be confused with similar forms of deterioration in ivory.

5 Modifications of Animal Materials

So much of an animal's life history is reflected in its bones, as its behaviors and dietary patterns can alter aspects of the body on a skeletal level. In some cases, these changes are independent of human activities: Deer often create abrasions on their antlers as a result of shedding velvet or fighting with others during the mating season. Likewise, certain taxa (e.g., rodents, suids, and hippopotami) have continuously growing teeth that grind against each other, creating smooth wear facets that look like cut surfaces. Humans can also affect the skeletal development of animals through a variety of actions. For example, using domesticated animals for traction or transportation can create recognizable skeletal markers. Draft animals often develop excess ossification in their toe bones from pulling heavy loads, while animals that were harnessed and ridden using a bit will show distinct patterns of tooth wear.

Humans also directly alter animal skeletons through hunting, butchery, cooking, and the creation of worked animal objects. These modifications might take a variety of forms, including a cut surface, a hack mark, or a drill hole. Skeletal materials modified because of dietary practices may be discarded and deposited fairly quickly, while worked animal objects might circulate for hundreds of years. Through prolonged use or display, these objects may become abraded or polished. After animal materials are deposited, a host of taphonomic processes further alter them. Contact with metals may stain large portions of skeletal materials, while acidic soils might wholly eradicate keratinous materials like horn or baleen.

As a result of all these factors, researchers studying worked animal objects must attempt to distinguish among modifications of skeletal materials resulting from factors that occurred during the animal's life; anthropogenic modifications related to dietary practices; the actions of craftspeople creating worked animal objects; changes to these objects related to their use, and the effects of taphonomic processes. To complicate matters, worked animal objects may exhibit multiple features resulting from separate processes, as animal materials used by craftspeople may have been sourced from butchered dietary refuse. In many cases, it is easy to recognize that an animal material has been modified. Cut marks render the curves of skeletal material into unnaturally flat surfaces and straight lines; decorative designs like the ring-and-dot motif sharply contrast against an organic medium. However, these materials are subject to a variety of different processes between the start of the animal's life and the deposition and recovery of the worked animal object.

It is often challenging to associate a modification of a worked animal object with a particular tool. Such a characterization relies on a thorough understanding of the production environment. Moreover, technologies used by craftspeople vary among different cultures and time periods; individuals in the Paleolithic approached a material like bone with different tools and methods than the craftspeople of the medieval period. Moreover, technologies are socially determined practices, meaning that individuals make decisions about how to alter animal materials with respect to their experiences, training, and environment; craftspeople may choose to adopt or reject a technique or type of tool for social, rather than practical, reasons.

While it may be difficult to identify particular tools or techniques, there are a series of approaches that are broadly shared across crafting traditions. Creating worked animal objects primarily involves some sort of extractive or reductive process, in which the craftsperson uses several techniques (e.g., cutting, scraping, sawing, and drilling) to remove material to create a final product. Yet production does not begin with a pristine piece of bone or tooth; finished objects may appear polished, elegant, and exceptionally refined, but the beauty of the final products masks the reality of their organic, and often messy, origins. Demarcating the beginning of the production process is a subjective decision, as transforming a living animal into a worked object encompasses disparate technical practices (e.g., herding, hunting, slaughtering, and skinning). However, this Element examines the technical acts that were enacted primarily for the purpose of creating a worked animal object and which took place after the material was acquired.

5.1 Bone Surface Modification Unrelated to Craft Production

Acts of butchery, cooking, and food consumption all leave a variety of modifications on the surfaces of bone. Identifying and interpreting these modifications is frequently challenging and there can be ambiguity as to how or why such marks were made (James & Thompson 2015). Differentiating these modifications from the remains of worked bone production is similarly challenging. Moreover, there can be overlap between the types of modifications: Bone that was once butchered may be subsequently worked. A modification such as butchery will not always be clearly distinguishable from the production waste left by a craftsperson. The actions that produce these modifications are culturally mediated (e.g., the choice of tool, and the techniques used), meaning that the appearance of butchery marks and production waste will differ between societies. Deciding whether a worked animal object is the result of butchery, craft production, or some other practice requires an understanding and a familiarity with the culturally specific processes that create faunal assemblages, knowledge which is gained through experience.

Despite these challenges, there are some general principles that can help guide the decision-making process. As R. Lee Lyman (Lyman 1994, 301) points out, butchery marks are epiphenomena, unintended side effects of other actions. In contrast, the modifications created by craftspeople are the intentional results of the production process. As a result, the degree to which an animal material has been modified helps to determine whether it was the result of craft production. A higher degree of modification generally corresponds to craft production, as butchery and cooking practices are primarily concerned with extracting meat rather than cutting it into bone. A piece of bone exhibiting substantial modification on multiple surfaces is more likely to be a piece of production waste or an unfinished object than the remains of butchery. Similarly, modifications which appear planned, deliberate, and which do not seem to serve any purpose related to food preparation are more likely to be the result of crafting actions. However, evidence for the extraction of fat or marrow is not rare in the archaeological record, and these processes result in extensive modifications to bone (e.g., crushing, splitting, and splintering). These actions may leave behind scraps of modified bone that appear similar to tools (i.e., pseudo-tools). So, in addition to observing the degree to which a bone has been altered, researchers also have to interpret both the extent and the nature of the modification.

While butchery varies among cultures and time periods, there are some relatively common practices that result in modified bones that are recognizable as products of food preparation. Butchers often divide the animal carcass into halves, cutting through the vertebral column in the process. Likewise, rib bones are also likely to be cut during the butchery or cooking process. As a result, split vertebrae and ribs with single cut marks are common in many dietary assemblages. The presence of small shallow cut marks (i.e., fillet marks) on otherwise unmodified pieces of bone are generally indicative of food preparation as well. Small cut marks at the articulation points between elements result from butchers separating the limbs of the animal into smaller cuts of meat. Similar marks are also found on other surfaces of the bone, often a result of cooking or dining practices (e.g., scraping the bone while cutting off a portion of meat). The presence of these marks does not disqualify a bone from being used in craft production, as worked skeletal elements were often subject to the same disarticulation processes. As with other aspects of the study of worked animal objects, it is important for researchers to be forthright about their decision-making process and their confidence in an attribution. If the modifications found on bone are ambiguous, researchers should record that an object may be the result of butchery or craft production.

5.2 Preparatory Techniques

The initial stages of the production of worked animal objects often involved preparing the material for subsequent modifications. Soft tissues (e.g., tendons, and ligaments) attached to osseous materials would have needed to be removed. Bone, antler, ivory, and keratinous materials can also be hard, inflexible, and difficult to modify. While some preparatory techniques may be of an extractive or reductive nature (e.g., cutting tendons from the surface of the bone), many also involve soaking, heating, or desiccation to alter the chemical and physical properties of the material. As marrow and other organic fluids can remain encased in the organic matrix of the bone, craftspeople may have also chosen to degrease the material by boiling it in water. Bone fats provided a valuable resource in many societies; however, most fat exploitation involves fracturing large amounts of bone into small pieces, with an emphasis on the nutrient-rich trabecular regions. As a result, the preparatory method of boiling bone for craft production was likely separate from processes of dietary fat exploitation. Boiling had an additional advantage of making bone and antler softer and easier to manipulate. Experimental research demonstrates that using softened bone and antler is significantly less stressful on stone tools (Osipowicz 2007). Additionally, boiling is not the only method of making osseous materials more pliable, as experimental research shows that soaking these materials in liquids with favorable chemical properties (usually an acidic solution) can make them easier to carve. Experimental and ethnographic research demonstrates that bone and antler can be softened using sour milk, urine, water mixed with sorrel, water mixed with ashes, and oil (Osipowicz 2007, 3).

Craftspeople subjected proboscidean ivory to similar chemical processes to soften and mold the material, including boiling in wine, heating in fire, and soaking in vinegar or beer (Lapatin 2001, 75–77). Similar methods were used to prepare horn, which was soaked in water or some other liquid to remove the outer keratin layer from the horn core. Craftspeople also used desiccation to dry out the organic bonds that held together the horn and horn core. Once the horn was removed from the horn core, craftspeople applied heat to help soften the material before cutting it open (MacGregor 1985, 66–67). Methods of soaking, boiling, and desiccating animal materials may have been a standard aspect of the production process for many craftspeople, but these techniques leave little archaeological signature and are unlikely to be detected from observing animal materials alone.

5.3 Extractive-Reductive Techniques

Creating worked animal objects requires changing the shape of an existing organic structure, so nearly all modifications of animal materials involve an extractive or reductive method. Trying to differentiate between these techniques reflects, to some extent, an artificial separation between overlapping actions. Incising the surface of a bone may simultaneously involve a degree of sawing and abrasion. Similarly, drilling techniques often comprise actions of abrasion and cutting. As a result, attempting to characterize production techniques represents a schematized way of presenting information. While the following groups of techniques are imperfect categories, they represent a means of thinking about and ordering the many ways craftspeople modified animal materials in the past.

5.3.1 Incision

Incision involves the use of a tool (e.g., knife, gouge, and awl) to cut into the surface of the material to a limited depth. Incised lines differ in appearance: They can be straight or curved, carved freehand or with a fixed tool, and the depth of the incision varies depending on the object or craft. For example, scrimshanders incised very fine lines as a way of illustrating and shading scenes on the surfaces of whale teeth. The technique of incision was also used to create larger lines at a greater depth (see Figure 2). One of the most widespread motifs found on worked animal materials is the ring-and-dot pattern, which consists of an outer circle (ring) surrounding an incised or impressed circular region (dot). The ring-and-dot motif is achieved using a scribing tool, a pronged metal object that cuts into the material at a fixed radius. Craftspeople could use scribing tools of different sizes to create patterns with multiple rings enclosing the same central dot, a pattern akin to a "bullseye." Compasses or scribing tools could also be used to create patterns of interconnected arcs, such as the guilloche pattern or the hexafoil motif. Figure 2 shows both incised lines and the ring-and-dot motif. The profile of incised lines may differ depending on what tool was used, but generally these lines present as a narrow, V-shaped or U-shaped valley. Additionally, this technique generally leaves behind the same amount of material on either side of the incised line.

5.3.2 Knapping

The process of knapping is a technique of breaking away sections of a material using a percussive tool. Knapping is strongly associated with lithic technologies, but a similar approach was also been used for animal materials. Knapped lithic materials have a series of distinct features, including the presence of a force cone and compression waves. When the knapper strikes the stone, the force propagates through the material in a wave, creating cone or bulb like formations. The flake is sheared away, often preserving ripples of force on the exposed surface (compression waves). Stone is very different from animal materials, meaning that knapping will not necessarily produce the same effects. However, these distinct visual characteristics have been detected among antler and ivory production waste at prehistoric sites in Europe and Asia (Heckel & Wolf 2014; Girya & Khlopachev 2019, 326). Worked animal materials exhibiting rounded faces that were sheared away and which show lines of force radiating through the material in the form of small bands are evidence for knapping techniques. Knapping may also leave an archaeological signature in the form of the flakes of bone or antler that were removed. In their exploration of the production of antler objects found a rock shelter in France, Aline Averbouh and Jean-Marc Pétillon (2009) observed several flakes that were unworked and smaller than finished objects in the assemblage. They conclude that craftspeople at the site were knapping to sectioning the antler ("debitage by fracturation"). However, it can be difficult to identify bone and antler objects created through knapping, as a minimally worked tool created from a flake of bone will look very similar to other pieces of unmodified bone in the assemblage. Additionally, the potential for identifying "pseudo-tools" is high, as many processes result in the deposition of broken bones which are visually similar to tools that were purposefully made. Moreover, knapping may be an initial or intermediate step in the production process, after which subsequent actions (e.g., abrasion) may remove traces of this technique.

5.3.3 Splitting Techniques

There are a series of techniques that involve cutting a groove in the osseous material to create a fracture point. Subsequently, the craftsperson applies a force to separate the material in a controlled manner. Similar techniques appear in other technological traditions (e.g., lithic manufacture) and have been found across cultures and time periods. These methods have variously been referred to as "groove-and-snap," "groove-twist-snap," "cut-and-break," as well as "chop-and-snap" techniques. Evidence for these techniques is often found among societies that relied primarily on stone tools, and these approaches appear to have been more economical than cutting through the material. However, there is no reason that metal tools could not have been used within these practices as well. Grooving methods can be applied to both the transverse and longitudinal axes, either as a means of preparing sections for subsequent modification or to remove undesirable portions of the animal material. When this technique is used along the transverse axis, such as around the base of an antler tine, the craftsperson may be able to break off the material using their hands. Snapping techniques along a transverse axis can leave a recognizable feature: a spur of material that juts out beyond the grooved surface. While this feature can be a diagnostic aspect of the technique, subsequent production actions (e.g., abrasion or polish) may obscure the broken surface. Grooving techniques along the longitudinal axis rely on the same principle. Evidence for a technique of creating points from the bones of small mammals and birds was found within assemblages in southern Louisiana. Based on experimental data, Dave Davis and collaborators (1983, 100) surmise that the craftspeople began by incising the shape of the point into the bone and then broke it by employing "major sheer stress" to the transverse axis while applying a "slight twist."

Using small and pliable bones, it is possible to split longitudinal sections with bare hands. However, longitudinal splitting may also require a percussive force (e.g., a hammer, hitting the material against an anvil) to split the material. Alice Choyke and Zsuzsanna Tóth (2013, 344) describe their experimental approach to splitting grooved metapodials, writing that "the action consists of gentle movements. The aim is to crack the bone along the prepared line with the chisel acting as wedge." In this case, there is some overlap between the different actions, as Choyke and Tóth used the grooving tool to separate the bone. The "groove-and-splinter" technique also relies on creating fracture points, but it is used to extract longitudinal portions from a core of osseous material and is most strongly associated with Paleolithic antler objects (Clark & Thompson 1954; Semenov 1964, 155–158; Zhilin 1998; Pétillon & Ducasse 2012; Baumann & Maury 2013). Using this method, the craftsperson cuts parallel grooves into the material in the longitudinal direction. Subsequently, the craftsperson uses a tool to pry out the portion of the material between the parallel grooves. This technique produces long, straight sections of antler that can be subsequently worked into points.

5.3.4 Abrasion

Abrasion is the act of changing the shape or appearance of an object through extended contact with another material. One application of this technique involves moving the animal material over a coarse surface (e.g., stone) to level and smooth the material. This method was often used to create flat surfaces (e.g., scrapers), and the same technique was used to create a point from a series of angled surfaces. The points could be further refined by rotating the point against the coarse surface, creating a rounded tip. Unlike a cut surface, the abraded surface displays more obvious irregularities. Unless subsequently polished, abraded animal materials will display striations from the production action. If abrasion was used to create a flat edge (e.g., a scraper), the striations may be oriented in roughly the same direction. However, using abrasion to create a rounded point entails moving the material in multiple directions, changing the orientations of the striations.

Abrasive techniques are also used to polish animal materials: Softer materials like leather or fine sand can give worked animal objects a smooth and shiny surface. While worked animal objects often exhibit polish, this feature may be a deliberate technique of the craftsperson (Figure 27B) or the result of some other process. Objects that consistently come into contact with human hands

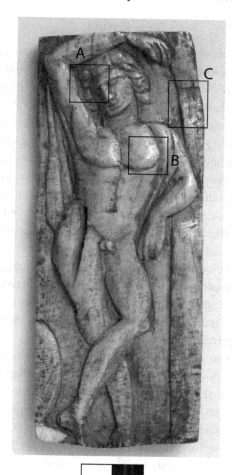

Figure 27 Hellenistic bone carving of Dionysos. (A) Negative space created by carving. (B) Shine from polish. (C) Chisel marks showing circular pitting and striations on the cut surface. (ca. fourth–sixth centuries CE).

Source: Metropolitan Museum of Art, accession number: 1993.516.1.

(e.g., tool handles) can inadvertently become polished. Moreover, objects that are suspended or affixed by a rope or cord may also become abraded and polished through use; Figure 9 shows wear around the drill hole that originated from use. Using evidence of polish as criteria for determining whether an object is worked can also pose a challenge because the burial environment can abrade animal materials over time, making the material appear anthropogenically modified (e.g., Thorson & Guthrie 1984; Fisher 1995, 34–36). Polished surfaces are typified by a smooth feeling and a degree of shine, although taphonomic factors can also obscure these features.

5.3.5 Drilling

Drilling techniques represent a common means of perforating animal materials. The rapid rotation of a drill forms a hole by cutting into or abrading the animal material. Drills were often made from metal or stone but have also been constructed using other materials. Craftspeople may have also added abrasive materials like fine sand or emery powder during the drilling process. Drilling methods and technologies also varied between cultures and time periods, as innovations like the bow drill and pump drill allowed for faster and more constant motion. Different methods of drilling can result in holes that vary in appearance, although drill holes will often exhibit a uniform diameter throughout. Owing to differences in drilling techniques, there can be some uncertainty in determining whether a hole was made by a drill or other method. A uniform diameter is a strong indication that a hole was made by a drill, although variations in drilling techniques or the skill of the craftsperson might create uneven drill holes. Craftspeople wishing to perforate an animal material without a drill will often cut into the surface of the animal material from two sides, resulting in an hourglass-shaped perforation; holes made with this technique will generally show two uneven piercings that narrow toward the center.

Drilling can also serve as an extractive method to remove portions of material to be subsequently worked. Using a tubular drills, craftspeople can remove a section of the animal material, which might be turned into an object like a button or a ring. It can be difficult to identify finished objects created from a material that was extracted using a drill, as traces of the process might be completely obscured in the final product. The best evidence for the use of extractive drilling techniques is often only visible in the production waste; this waste might present as a piece of animal material with a series of circular holes (Bikić & Vitezović 2016). Craftspeople drilling into thicker skeletal elements might leave behind circular concavities which feature a spur of broken bone from the center.

5.3.6 Lathe

A lathe is a device that rapidly turns a material around an axis of rotation, allowing a craftsperson to remove small amounts of that material using a cutting tool. Lathes produce objects that are highly symmetrical about the axis of rotation, allowing craftspeople to create spherical, grooved, and tapered shapes. Determining whether a lathe was used to create an object can be challenging because this technique leaves behind ephemeral production waste that does not preserve within the archaeological record (i.e., shavings). Additionally, skilled craftspeople in the past were able to create symmetrical objects without using turning tools, so an even appearance is not necessarily a good indication of the use of a lathe. However, materials cut using a lathe tend to leave behind a series of regular striations resulting from cutting tools contacting the surface of the material; these marks are visible to the naked eye and perpendicular to the axis of rotation (see Figure 3). Lathes can also be used in association with abrasive methods to produce a high degree of polish.

5.3.7 Sawing

The technique of sawing involves using a tool in a back-and-forth motion to cut into an animal material; the cutting action either occurs in both directions or is unidirectional. Some sawing actions are primarily abrasive, using the surface of the tool and potentially an additional substance (e.g., fine sand, emery powder) to wear away the material. Using an abrasive method, experimental recreations of sandstone saws have been able to cut into a variety of materials, including whale bone (Kendig et al. 2010, 202–203). Additionally, experimental studies also demonstrated that using a string saw in conjunction with an abrasive substance was nearly as efficient as a serrated bronze knife for cutting into bone (Wang et al. 2022, 9). Other types of saws have sharpened or serrated edges to cut into the material. Each movement of the sawing tool leaves striations on the surface of the animal material that are generally visible to the naked eye. When craftspeople change the orientation of the tool, the striations also change direction. Saw mark striations can be seen on Figures 1 and 25; Figure 1 shows changes in the orientation of the striations closest to bone spur on the example on the left. Saw mark patterns can be somewhat ambiguous, as changes in cutting orientation result in the striations intersecting at different angles. When an object exhibits an incomplete saw mark, it appears as a valley-shaped area that has a roughly even amount of material on either side (Figure 13A). Incomplete saw marks are valuable for understanding the production process, so researchers should attempt to describe their width and profile (e.g., V-shaped, rectangular) because these features will differ depending on the tool used.

Sawing actions can leave behind features that are separate from the cutting motion itself. When a craftsperson sawing through an object nears the end of the cut, the small amount of material remaining can break easily. Either the craftsperson chooses to snap away the last portion or the pressure on the material causes it to break apart. The result of this action is either a protruding spur or small concavity. In the left example of a cut metapodial in Figure 1, a small spur shows where the cutting action terminated. While the presence of spurs is associated with all techniques that involve snapping, small spurs on otherwise neat surfaces are strong indications of a cutting or sawing action.

5.3.8 Hacking or Chopping

As opposed to the controlled method of separating animal materials with a saw, hacking is the act of cutting into a material using a series of striking or chopping motions in which the blade is moved perpendicular to its cutting edge (i.e., an up-and-down motion rather than a side-to-side motion). Hacking or chopping actions can be completely perpendicular to the material (i.e., used to split a material in two parts). Alternatively, hacking or chopping motions can also be performed parallel to the surface, shearing off small amounts of material and leaving behind a flat cut surface. When hacking or chopping is performed with metal tools, this action can leave behind a flat surface or cutting plane that forms when the material is sheared away. In this case, the tool can leave striations on that cut surface that follows the direction of the striking action. As hack marks are usually achieved in a single motion, there is less variation among the direction of the striations on the cut surface. However, stone tools do not possess enough of a uniform edge to leave behind this sheared face. Experimental studies have shown that stone tools tend to cause "splintering and fragmentation on both sides of the chop" (Okaluk & Greenfield 2022, 23). Moreover, all tools can cause a degree of crushing, a deformation of the animal material that often appears similar to other taphonomic processes. As a result, complete chop marks made with stone tools can be difficult to identify. However, Tiffany Okaluk and Haskel Greenfield (2022, 18) note that hack marks made with stone tools produced associated "peck marks," areas of irregular deformation around the cutting surface. Depending on the angle of the cut, the size of the tool, and the nature of the material, incomplete hack marks made with metal tools can appear similar to an incomplete saw mark (i.e., valley-shaped), although signs of crushing or shearing are indications that the mark was made with a chopping action. Hacking or chopping can be a less controlled action, so there is a tendency for craftspeople to strike the material more than once, resulting in multiple marks at similar orientations. In Figure 9, there are a series of hack marks made at a slight downward angle. These marks have a series of sheared surfaces that show where the blade struck the material.

5.3.9 Scraping or Chiseling

Using a tool with a cutting edge like a knife, chisel, or gouge, the craftsperson can scrape the surface to remove material or create a flat face. These cutting actions are the result of the craftsperson applying consistent force parallel to the surface, altering the material without cutting too deeply. While sawing actions tend to leave behind obvious striations, scraping tools produce different types of marks. The cut surface can appear sheared, such as what occurs when a metal

Figure 28 Antler fibula plate from ancient Methone, with
and without raking light.
Source: Photographs by Jeff Vanderpool.

tool is used to chop. However, a chisel or similar tool may form small linear marks perpendicular to the cutting surface. These marks represent the results of the craftsperson attempting to apply consistent force to the cutting action. If the tool hits a thicker portion of the material and can not cut any farther, it will leave behind these linear marks (Figure 27C). Flat-cutting tools may also leave behind rounded marks that appear as small gouges within the material; such marks are visible in Figure 27 (Area marked C and elsewhere). Scraping or chiseling can also produce a distinct tool mark called "chatter." Chatter is a result of a craftsperson applying too much pressure for the angle of the tool. If there is insufficient lubrication between the material and the tool, the material will vibrate from the force of the tool. As the material vibrates, the tool bounces off and strikes the surface periodically, creating a banded pattern. Chatter is marked by a strong regularity which may make them appear as though they were the result of a deliberate action. Chatter marks also tend to be shallow and may not be visible in all lighting conditions. The surface of the object in Figure 28 shows scraping or chiseling tool marks, including a small amount of chatter on the bottom half.

5.3.10 Carving

Carving is a reductive process, in which the craftsperson removes material to create a shape or design. As a result, carving might represent several different production techniques (e.g., drilling, incision, or the use of a knife), some of which may not leave any trace. Referring to an object as "carved" recognizes that the object underwent significant extractive-reductive techniques to create its current shape, meaning that it is really a composite of different techniques. Carving creates areas of negative space and is often used to create sculpture and relief. Identifying carving requires understanding the original dimensions of the material, as the highest surfaces of a carving will represent areas where the least amount of material was removed. In Figure 27A, there is clear use of negative space between two raised areas. This indicates that the craftsperson used extractive techniques to shape this region.

6 Studying Animal Materials

The previous section provide a description of the morphology of animal materials and an overview of the methods used by craftspeople to create worked animal objects. Using these concepts, archaeological researchers can study individual worked animal objects in the field or museum settings. However, there are a host of issues that can impact the interpretation of the assemblage as a whole, and researchers studying museum collections or objects from past excavations must understand the limitations of the data set. Objects in a museum collection may only represent the most conspicuous finds rather than a representative sample of what was excavated. Moreover, worked animal objects can be easily neglected on an archaeological excavation: Zooarchaeologists may separate them from the rest of the faunal assemblage, treating the materials as they would other artifacts. Some zooarchaeologists analyze these finds, while others feel that it is the purview of an artifact specialist. Not every artifact specialist feels qualified to study worked animal objects, so they can remain unanalyzed. Furthermore, worked animal materials can be difficult to identify within the field, so a significant portion may remain unidentified within the faunal assemblage. As some excavations lack dedicated zooarchaeologists, and the process of faunal identification can be time-consuming, there is further potential for worked animal materials to be unidentified.

Researchers studying materials from past excavations may be stymied by the challenges of working with data that is not being collected actively. Depending on the protocols of the past excavation, archaeologists may have only saved objects they deemed important or representative. As a result, it is incumbent on the researcher to try to understand and articulate to the degree to which an assemblage is incomplete (i.e., study previous excavation notes). Without fully comprehending how worked animal objects were recovered, researchers are severely limited in their abilities to interpret the production environment, the abilities or skills of the craftspeople, and the degree to which an animal material is typical or unique. When examining only a limited subset of what was originally excavated, it becomes nearly impossible to make larger inferences about the practices that resulted in the assemblage under consideration. These issues can be further compounded by inadequate storage, as worked animal objects that were not properly separated from a faunal assemblage can become fragmented, broken, or abraded. Researchers should ascertain how many worked animal objects were recovered during excavation. If the unworked faunal assemblage is not fully analyzed, the researcher should attempt to examine as much of this material as possible. However, there may be so much faunal material that a comprehensive study is impossible. In that case, researchers should adopt a sampling strategy to examine a representative portion.

For researchers conducting a study of a worked animal assemblage of an active or recent excavation project, communication with the zooarchaeologist, conservation specialists, and the excavation supervisors is necessary for establishing a protocol for handling, storing, and studying these materials. Before beginning a study, researchers need to resolve the following issues:

- What percentage of the faunal assemblage has been cleaned and analyzed?
- Are worked animal materials that have already been identified stored separately from the rest of the faunal assemblage?
- If previously unidentified worked animal materials are found within the faunal assemblage, what is the procedure for creating a new ID/artifact number?
- What counts as a worked animal material? Should horn core with cut marks count as a worked animal material or a byproduct of butchery?
- Will the faunal specialist record any information about the worked animal materials?
- Are the excavators sampling deposits for the purpose of flotation? Who is responsible for sorting and analyzing the fractions?

Researchers studying materials from an active excavation have the advantage of being able to witness the faunal assemblage as it comes out of the ground. After it has been cleaned, faunal material provides insight into general taphonomic processes that may be affecting the assemblage. Moreover, examining the faunal assemblage during excavation can be a way of identifying worked animal materials that were missed in the field. For excavations utilizing flotation, researchers should examine faunal material found in the light fraction. Animal materials are very common in the light fraction, so it is difficult to identify fragments of worked bone with certainty, as these pieces may also be the remains of butchery. However, certain types of ivory may be identifiable at a small scale. Such pieces may be the waste products of the craft production process, offering insight into the nature of the archaeological context. A proactive approach to studying materials in the field can result in a greater understanding of how worked animal objects were created and can lead to better excavation practices.

Worked animal objects recovered in the field need to be cleaned, preferably after developing protocols with a conservation specialist. These objects can be prone to fragmentation or delamination, so the cleaning methods used for ceramics or unworked faunal materials may be unsuitable. Bone objects without signs of degradation can often be washed with a soft brush or a cotton swab and a small amount of water, although dry brushing is a less invasive technique that is adequate for removing dirt from the surface of the material. Antler frequently has preservation issues, so if the surface appears crumbly or chalky, it should not be submerged in water. Objects made of ivory are also sensitive to changes in moisture and can become delaminated easily, so they should not be cleaned aggressively. Similarly, objects made from teeth which retain enamel may also be at risk of fragmentation, as the enamel layer is often thin; objects showing cracks in the enamel should be handled with caution. As keratin is especially prone to decomposition, any such objects recovered in an excavation must be treated by a conservation specialist. Regardless of the material, the move from the burial environment to the open air will mean that the object is exposed to a different level of humidity. As a result, researchers need to make sure objects are sufficiently dry before they are placed in bags for storage.

6.1 Observation and Recording

After the researcher has located and cleaned all the worked animal objects under consideration, it is time to begin making observations. Researchers studying worked animal objects should employ a bright flashlight or LED light, a simple lens (e.g., a 10x jeweler's loupe), plastic calipers (metal calipers are prone to damaging the surface of worked animal materials), a digital scale, and a camera (with scale bar). A hand-held digital microscope is also helpful for recognizing and documenting anatomical structures and anthropogenic modifications.

Recording and understanding contextual information is an essential aspect of any archaeological analysis, although objects from museum collections may lack such information. It is essential to record as much of the contextual and excavation-related information as possible (e.g., archaeological context, date recovered, and bag number). Researchers examining bulk-collected assemblages of faunal materials may discover previously unrecognized worked animal objects. These objects need to be removed from the faunal assemblage, but it is imperative that no information is lost; it should be possible to reassociate these objects with the bulk collected faunal material from which they were removed. In addition to contextual information, researchers should record measurements, taxonomic information, taphonomic information, and a thorough written descriptions of the modifications and the object itself.

The purpose of the written description is not to produce a text ready for a publication or catalog, but to capture a range of observations about the object under study. The researcher should try to convey their thoughts about how the object was modified and whether there are any signs of use wear. This description will likely repeat information recorded elsewhere, but this text is a way of creating a narrative about the object. It is a place for ideas, inferences, and theories. It is a form of note-taking that will evolve with the study of each subsequent object. By taking a more maximal approach to description and observation, researchers ensure that they will not overlook important details. Moreover, this text provides a basis for writing more formalized object descriptions for publication. Researchers should record details about the different types of modified surfaces on the object. Some modifications are the result of actions taken by the craftsperson, while others occur through the handling of the object (i.e., use wear). A description of a modification should detail its appearance and the type of anthropogenic action which may have caused it:

- *The proximal face of the astragalus appears roughly flat, with a smooth a slightly shiny surface. This is likely a result of the craftsperson abrading the bone in multiple directions.*
- *The distal end of a cattle metapodial has a smooth cut face with small striations that are all oriented at the same angle, seemingly the result of a craftsperson using a saw to cut through the bone.*
- *A shiny teardrop-shaped area around the drill hole, presumably the result of a cord abrading the bone through use.*

CHECKLIST FOR STUDYING WORKED ANIMAL MATERIALS

- Source of light (Flashlight or LED lamp)
- Simple lens
- Plastic calipers
- Digital scale
- Camera
- Scale bar
- Recording system/Database

6.1.1 Quantification and Recording Techniques

Researchers need to consider how the choice of quantification strategy will affect the interpretation of the archaeological assemblage. Adopting a quantification strategy akin to the number of identified specimens (NISP) metric in zooarchaeology (i.e., each fragment is counted as a single unit) may be appropriate for certain assemblages. However, a metric like NISP can be disadvantageous when the assemblage is highly fragmented. As in zooarchaeology, counting each fragment has the ability to overrepresent the quantity of materials that were initially deposited. It is important for the researcher to decide on a procedure for studying horn core, as this material can be very common within the faunal assemblage, prone to fragmentation, and its presence in the archaeological record is not always the result of a craft production action. Within an archaeological assemblage, horn core might be both ubiquitous and predisposed to poor preservation, meaning that a researcher could end up quantifying several fragments originating from the same element. Moreover, most of the horn core is not likely to show evidence of anthropogenic modification (i.e., the horn core exhibits a transverse cut at the base and the rest of the element is unmodified). In this case, the researcher can choose to quantify only pieces of horn core showing evidence of modification. Such an approach might not be appropriate for other materials, such as elephant ivory. If the researcher is studying an assemblage in which elephant ivory is a product of long-distance trade, every fragment should be counted regardless of size or signs of modification. Researchers need to choose a quantification strategy that suits the assemblage they are studying. A good strategy will attempt to treat each worked animal object as a single unit, each with accompanying measurements and observations. Additionally, the risk of over-representing certain materials or objects can be countered by weighing each unit of observation.

Excavation projects assign identifying information to archaeological finds in several ways, for example certain objects may receive a "small finds" number, while others are collected in bulk. To study an assemblage of worked animal objects properly, each unit of observation needs to have a unique identifier. Therefore, it is often necessary for the researcher to maintain an independent system of recording, assigning ID numbers to both finished objects and scraps of production waste. Assemblages of worked animal materials can be large and varied, requiring a recording strategy that can keep track of quantitative (e.g., measurements) and qualitative data (e.g., descriptions). A database has many advantages for such research, as the data can be standardized, queried, easily shared, and exported into other file formats. Additionally, database software can associate and display images alongside the data, which aids in interpreting and classifying the assemblage. A simple relational database for recording information about worked animal objects might consist of three tables: *Worked Objects*, *Modifications*, and *Measurements*. Each object would have a single unique ID ("Main ID") on the *Worked Objects* table. This table would also have fields to record the taxon, the material type, observations about material type, a description, the archaeological context, and a count (usually equal to 1). Recording the measurements and observations of modifications requires separate tables, as there are multiple observations (e.g., different types of measurements) associated with a single object. The *Modifications* and *Measurements* tables will both have unique IDs (Modification ID and Measurement

ID) for each observation. In place of database software, a similar recording strategy can also be achieved with multiple spreadsheets (for examples of a relational database and spreadsheets, see supplementary files).

6.1.2 Photography

Depending on the time frame of the study and the size of the assemblage, researchers should aim to record several images of each object. In the context of archaeological sites and museums, traditional object photography tries to reflect accurately the color, scale, and shape of an object. Such photographs are appropriate for more general publications and catalogs, but this style of photography may be less effective for studying and documenting worked animal objects. So, in addition to more traditional photography, researchers should also take photographs that help explain the relationship between the orientation of the original animal material and the archaeological object. A top view of an object that captures the entirety of the cross section of a long bone shaft provides clear insight into how the object was created. Diagnostic features like the Schreger pattern of proboscidean ivory or secondary dentine of walrus ivory are also useful for conveying information about the species and the material, all of which will be useful to other researchers.

Researchers should also take photographs that highlight signs of modification. Documentation of cut marks, drill holes, and evidence of abrasion is useful for articulating the steps of the production process. However, the lighting used in traditional object photography may be insufficient for capturing these marks. The use of intense raking light can produce high-contrast images, which make tool marks and other modifications stand out (see Figure 28). Keeping the object in one position and taking a series of photographs with the light source at different orientations provides a way of documenting a range of modifications, and annotating these images can complement the written descriptions as well.

6.1.3 Measurements

Measurements for worked animal objects can be variable and dependent on the type of object. As the difference between "height" and "length" depends on how the object is oriented, measurements could easily differ between researchers. Unlike other types of archaeological objects that are more standardized, there is rarely a consensus about the types of measurements needed to study worked animal objects. As a result, it is important to be thorough and descriptive about how the measurements were taken. When recording a measurement, the researcher should accompany it with a description that would allow other researchers to understand the precise meaning of that measurement.

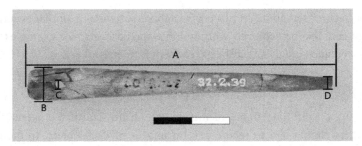

Figure 29 Ivory needle from northern Upper Egypt (ca. 4400–3800 BCE) showing types of measurements: The preserved length of the object, from finished end to broken end (A); the width of object at the finished end/width of object at the widest point (B); the diameter of drill hole nearest to the finished end (C), and the width of object at the broken point/width of object at the narrowest point (D).

Source: Metropolitan Museum of Art, accession number: 32.2.39.

Figure 29 shows a fragmentary ivory object with several measurements that aim to account accurately for the shape of the object. Descriptions of those measurements are as follows: the preserved length of the object, from finished end to broken end (A); the width of object at the finished end/width of object at the widest point (B); the diameter of drill hole nearest to the finished end (C), and the width of object at the broken point/width of object at the narrowest point (D). In addition, researchers should also measure the thickness of the object.

6.1.4 Taxonomy and Material Type

The biological aspects of worked animal objects, those traits normally studied by zooarchaeologists, are crucial for understanding how these objects were created and used in the past. Researchers unfamiliar with the study of animal bones should attempt to work with a zooarchaeologist, although such collaborations are not always possible. Without being able to consult with a specialist, researchers should attempt to record taxonomic information in a way that is responsible and transparent. Most worked bone objects are made from mammalian skeletal material, which is often distinguishable from that of birds, reptiles, and fish. However, many worked animal objects are the result of a significant alteration of the original material, often precluding a species-level identification. Unless absolutely certain of the origin of the material, researchers should opt for larger, more general taxonomic categories. For example, an object made from a metapodial may be identifiable as originating from an equid rather than a ruminant, but differentiating between donkey (*Equus asinus*) and horse (*Equus caballus*) can be challenging. Therefore, researchers should record that the object belonged to category like "equid" or "horse, onager, or donkey."

Even if it is not feasible to identify the species or make a more general taxonomic classification (e.g., order, family, and genus), it may still be possible to determine that an object came from an animal of a certain size, e.g., "large mammal" (e.g., red deer, cow, bear, or horse), "medium mammal" (e.g., sheep, goat, and pig), or "small mammal" (e.g., rodent, cat). If this approach is taken, it is incumbent on researchers to define clearly what constitutes "large," "medium," or "small." When nothing can be said about taxonomy, researchers should specify that the animal material is from an "indeterminate vertebrate."

Researchers should also attempt their best approximation of the material type. As material identification can be challenging, it is best to record the object with a more flexible description: "bone or elephant ivory," "bone or antler," "ivory (hippopotamus or elephant)," "ivory (non-elephant)." The challenges of differentiating types of materials make it more responsible and helpful for other researchers to describe an object with a flexible description, such as "bone or ivory." While this ambiguity may seem inexpert, it indicates to other researchers that the identifications are more likely to be accurate (if imprecise). More descriptive classifications can be disadvantageous for quantifying data, so researchers may also choose to record a more standardized set of terms for the purposes of creating charts and graphs (e.g., bone, ivory, antler, unknown). More ambiguous classifications (e.g., "bone or elephant ivory," "bone or antler") would fall under the "unknown" category for the purposes of quantification. In the case of objects made from bone, it is also beneficial to record information about the skeletal element. Significantly carved bone objects can be impossible to identify, so researchers should opt for the best possible approximation of the element, e.g., "unknown," "long bone or metapodial," "phalanx 1 or 2." Classifications should be accompanied by notes on the characteristics or metrics used in the decision-making process.

- *The object exhibits the unmodified distal end of a ruminant metapodial. Based on the size and morphology, it likely originates from a sheep, goat, or fallow deer.*
- *The object is made from proboscidean ivory based on the appearance of the Schreger pattern visible on one of the cut surfaces.*
- *The material seems to be bone or antler, as it exhibits both cortical and trabecular skeletal tissue.*
- *The material is unknown, although likely some type of tooth because it shows no diagnostic signs of bone (e.g., Haversian canals, trabecular tissue).*
- *The object was carved from the diaphysis (shaft) of a long bone.*

6.1.5 Taphonomy

Skeletal materials are prone to multiple forms of deterioration and degradation in the burial environment, so recognizing the effects of taphonomic processes on animal materials is another important aspect of the recording process. The study of such taphonomic processes is an entire subfield of zooarchaeology (see Lyman 1994; Fernández-Jalvo & Andrews 2016), so researchers may be unfamiliar with the range of different alterations to skeletal materials. Moreover, there are taphonomic processes which mimic effects of production and use (e.g., abrasion), so researchers should take note of the surface or condition of the animal material which may not be the result of anthropogenic actions. A variety of other taphonomic factors may affect the appearance of worked animal objects. Such objects may have small, irregular marks caused by the gnawing of rodents or the growth of plant roots. There are also factors that can discolor animal materials, including metal staining, chemicals in the deposit, or fungal growth. Additionally, exposure to sunlight or moisture can negatively impact the surfaces of worked animal materials. Unfamiliarity with faunal materials may make identifying specific signatures of taphonomic processes difficult, so researchers should write a general description of the condition and color of the worked animal object.

WRITTEN OBSERVATIONS OF A WORKED ANTLER OBJECT

ID Number: 1
Context: Square A1, Context 100, Pass 3
Measurements: Length (Finished end with drill hole to broken end): 0.058 m; Width (widest point): 0.03 m; Diameter (drill hole): 0.005 m; Weight: 28.3 g.
Taxon: Cervid, likely red deer (*Cervus elaphus*).
Taphonomic Observations: Metal staining.
Material: Antler
Material Description: Interior exhibits a trabecular structure and the exterior has a ridged appearance that is characteristic of antler.
Description: An object made from a highly polished, cylindrical portion of antler. A hole was drilled through the antler on one end, and the other was roughly cut and is stained with iron; the areas of iron staining appear slightly raised in some areas. The cut marks are a series of hacks that go around the circumference of the object. The underside shows that the trabecular interior has a small hole in it, it is unclear whether this is an anthropogenic modification or a result of taphonomy. This surface also

has more iron staining. In addition to the polish on the outside surface, there is also an abraded and polished area around the drill hole. This abrasion suggests that the drill hole was used as a suspension loop, and that some sort of cord caused the abrasion. The hack marks are better defined and do not exhibit any abrasion, suggesting that the wear predates the cut marks. Perhaps this object represents the remains of a handle or haft that had been broken.

Modified Surfaces

Polish: The surface of the object has a polished appearance, although it is not wholly uniform. It is not clear whether the polish developed through use or was a deliberate choice by the craftsperson who created this object.

Cut Surface (Figure 9, A): The flat surface nearest to the drill hole represents where this portion of antler was cut from the rest of the beam. The surface has a flat facet that slants downward, suggesting that it was cut at multiple angles. However, the surface was subsequently abraded and there are not clear remains of cut marks.

Fine Cut Marks/Incisions (Figure 9, B): A series of fine incised lines cover the object, which are oriented at a variety of angles. The polished surface appears to go over these lines, suggesting that they were made at the time the object was created or during the time it was used.

Drill Hole (Figure 9, C): A uniform drill hole that goes through the width of the object.

Hack Marks (Figure 9, D): There are a series of cuts at a slight downward angle on one side of the object. These cut marks go around the object, surrounding a smaller spur of the trabecular portion of the antler. It seems likely that the extant portion of the object was snapped off a larger piece of antler after the cut marks were made (akin to a groove-and-snap technique). The cut marks appear to have been created in single downward strokes (i.e., a hack), as they lack the striations that are characteristic of a sawing or cutting action.

6.2 Identifying Animal Materials Using Scientific Analysis

While most studies of worked animal objects are conducted using the techniques outlined above, scientific analysis has become increasingly common for material identification. The development of Zooarchaeology by Mass Spectrometry (ZooMS) has resulted in a minimally destructive method for the identification of the genus (and sometimes species) of a wide range of animal materials. The ZooMS is an application of the techniques of proteomics, which use matrix-assisted laser desorption/ionization time-of-flight (MALDI-TOF) Mass Spectrometry to characterize peptides found within collagen. Due to the abundance of collagen in animal tissue, this method has been successfully applied to bone, ivory, baleen, tortoiseshell, horn, and soft materials like leather and fur. The ZooMS is a rapidly developing analytical technique that has become increasingly common in archaeological research because of its relatively inexpensive costs and small sample requirements (Richter et al. 2022). Researchers have also developed nondestructive applications of ZooMS methods; peptides were successfully analyzed from the inside of a plastic bag and from a PVC eraser that had been in contact with archaeological materials (McGrath et al. 2019). The analysis of ancient DNA (aDNA) has also been used to determine the genetic origin of worked animal objects, providing even more precise results than ZooMS. However, aDNA analysis requires a significantly larger sample size than ZooMS and the costs are higher. Nondestructive analysis using Fourier transform infrared spectroscopy (FT-IR) and Raman spectroscopy has a long history outside of the study of material culture but has been adopted for the study of archaeological objects made from keratinous materials (Edwards et al. 1998a; Espinoza et al. 2007). These techniques have been used successfully to identify horn, hoof, and tortoiseshell. Additionally, there has been some success in using FT-IR to discriminate ivory from other animal materials (Edwards et al. 1998b; Smith & Clark 2004, 1155), although the spectra for different biological tissues are often very similar.

7 Conclusion

Worked animal objects represent a heterogeneous category of archaeological evidence made up of an equally varied set of materials. Bone, antler, teeth, and keratinous materials of various shapes and sizes have served as media for the creation of different types of material culture over the course of millennia. The varied corpus of worked animal objects reflects not only the diversity of life on the planet but also the wide range of relationships between humans and animals. The bones of birds and the teeth of elephants have very different origins and properties, yet both materials originated from a once-living being. Because of their connection to the animal world, these materials have great potential to acquire deep symbolic meanings and ritual roles within the societies that use them for the creation of objects. Worked animal materials were also a crucial medium for tools and other implements of everyday life. This often-overlooked category of archaeological materials has the potential to expand our knowledge of the past, allowing us to ask new questions about ancient economies, craft practices, and the relationships between humans and animals.

However, there are several barriers to the study of worked animal objects, including the difficulties involved in identifying materials. It can be challenging to recognize worked animal materials in the field, so a considerable number of objects may remain unrecognized until a zooarchaeologist analyzes the faunal assemblage. Faunal analysts may be able to identify these materials, but some zooarchaeologists view the study of worked animal objects as a separate subdiscipline. Additionally, guides and resources that cover worked animal materials are often biased toward the fauna that were exploited in particular regions or time periods. As a result, assemblages of worked animal objects are often only selectively studied and incompletely published. Despite these obstacles, this Element seeks to help researchers accurately record information about worked animal materials. Ideally, an archaeological researcher attempting to study worked animal objects should make an effort to gain an understanding of zooarchaeology before undertaking any research. To best understand animal materials, researchers must have extended exposure to both worked and unworked faunal assemblages. With the understanding that not every researcher can be an expert on animal materials, this guide advocates for a maximal approach to collecting data and note-taking. Of course, there are always practical demands of time and access that will prevent the researcher from performing the "perfect" analysis. Additionally, an overly exhaustive research strategy can become unmanageable and create too much data.

A dominant theme of this Element is caution. Researchers must be thoughtful about how they approach their study, making sure to familiarize themselves with how the animal materials were excavated and stored. Additionally, researchers should be cautious about making identifications of materials and modifications. Determining whether a piece of bone is worked or butchery waste is not always possible, while separating use wear from other taphonomic processes is similarly challenging. Worked animal materials are variable, and our understanding of their production is still developing. In order to create data that is helpful to future researchers, it is essential to be transparent about sources of uncertainty in the analysis and presentation of worked animal objects.

8 Further Reading

Keratinous Materials

O'Connor, S. et al. (2015). "Advances in identifying archaeological traces of horn and other keratinous hard tissues."
Pedersen, M. C. (2004). *Gem and Ornamental Materials of Organic Origin.*
Wang, B. et al. (2019). "Lessons from the Ocean: Whale Baleen Fracture Resistance."

Material Composition and Identification

Penniman, T. (1952). *Pictures of Ivory and Other Animal Teeth Bone and Antler.*

Jowsey, J. (1966). "Studies of Haversian systems in man and some animals."

Krzyszkowska, O. (1990). *Ivory and Related Materials: An Illustrated Guide.*

MacGregor, A. (1985). *Bone, Antler, Ivory and Horn.*

Espinoza, E. O., & Mann, M.-J. (1992). "Identification Guide for Ivory and Ivory Substitutes."

Ashby, S. (2005). "Bone and antler combs: Towards a methodology for the understanding of trade and identity in Viking Age England and Scotland."

O'Connor, S. (2016). "The COWISHT project: Enhancing the identification of artefact raw materials."

Baker, B. W. et al. (2020). "CITES Identification Guide for Ivory and Ivory Substitutes."

Proboscidean Ivory/Schreger Pattern

Espinoza, E. O. & Mann, M.-J. (1993). "The history and significance of the schreger pattern in proboscidean ivory characterization."

Raubenheimer, E. J. (1999). "Morphological aspects and composition of African elephant (*Loxodonta africana*) ivory."

Trapani, J. & Fisher, D. C. (2003). "Discriminating proboscidean taxa using features of the schreger pattern in tusk dentin."

Locke, M. (2008). "Structure of ivory."

Virág, A. (2012). "Histogenesis of the unique morphology of proboscidean ivory."

Production Techniques

Clark, J. G. D. & Thompson, M. W. (1954). "The groove and splinter technique of working antler in Upper Palaeolithic and Mesolithic Europe."

Semenov, S. (1964). *Prehistoric Technology: An Experimental Study of the Oldest Tools and Artefacts from Traces of Manufacture and Wear.*

Davis, D. D. et al. (1983). "Reduction analysis of simple bone industries: An example from the Louisiana Coastal Zone."

MacGregor, A. (1985). *Bone, Antler, Ivory and Horn.*

Pétillon, J.-M. & Ducasse, S. (2012). "From flakes to grooves: A technical shift in antlerworking during the last glacial maximum in southwest France."

Baumann, M. & Maury, S. (2013). "Ideas no longer written in antler."

Choyke, A. & Tóth, Z. (2013). "Practice makes perfect: Quartered metapodial awls in the Late Neolithic of Hungary."

Okaluk, T. R. & Greenfield, H. J. (2022). "Macroscopic chop mark identification on archaeological bone: An experimental study of chipped stone, ground stone, copper, and bronze axe heads on bone."

Taphonomy

Lyman, R. L. (1994). *Vertebrate Taphonomy*.
Fernández-Jalvo, Y. & Andrews, P. (2016). *Atlas of Taphonomic Identifications*.

Whale Bone

Betts, M. (2007). "The Mackenzie Inuit whale bone industry."
Pétillon, J.-M. (2013). "Circulation of whale-bone artifacts in the northern Pyrenees during the late Upper Paleolithic."

Worked Bone Research Group (WBRG)

The following are the publications of the WBRG (see introduction). Website: www.wbrg.net/.
Choyke, A. M. & Bartosiewicz, L., eds. (2001), *Crafting Bone: Skeletal Technologies through Time and Space*.
Riddler, I., ed. (2003), *Materials of Manufacture*.
Luik, H. et al., eds. (2005), *From Hooves to Horns, from Mollusc to Mammoth*.
St-Pierre, C. G. & Walker, R. B., eds. (2007), *Bones as Tools*.
Legrand-Pineau, A. et al., eds. (2010), *Ancient and Modern Bone Artefacts from America to Russia*.
Baron, J. & Kufel-Diakowska, B., eds. (2011), *Written in Bones*.
Lang, F., ed. (2013), *The Sound of Bones*.
Ma, X. & Hou, Y., eds. (2014), *Proceedings of the 9th Meeting of the (ICAZ) Worked Bone Research Group*.
Vitezović, S., ed. (2016), *Close to the Bone*.
Bejenaru, L., ed. (2018) 'Worked Bone and Archaeology,' *Quaternary International*.
González, F. M., ed. (2019) *Cuadernos de Prehistoria y Arqueología de la Universidad de Granada*.
Wild, M. et al., eds. (2021), *Bones at a Crossroads*.

Scientific Analysis of Animal Materials

Solazzo, C. et al. (2017). "Molecular markers in keratins from mysticeti whales for species identification of baleen in museum and archaeological collections."
Richter, K. K. et al. (2022). "A primer for ZooMS applications in archaeology."

Glossary

Baleen: The keratinous sheets that form in the mouths of Baleen whales and are used for filter feeding. This material was used for a variety of purposes, but rarely survives in the archaeological record.

Beam: The central stem of the antler.

Cementum: Dental tissue that often covers the roots of the teeth. Proboscidean tusks are almost entirely covered in cementum. It is sometimes referred to as the "bark" of the ivory.

Cementum-Dentine Junction: The interface between the cementum and dentine within the tooth. It can be a diagnostic feature of certain types of ivory, especially when viewed in transverse section.

Cone-within-Cone Splitting: The process of delamination that causes proboscidean ivory to split in layers that radiate from the center of the tooth.

Coronet: The ringed base of the antler which resembles a crown.

Cancellous Bone: Dense bone which helps to bear weight and give the skeleton strength. Large amounts of cancellous bone can be found in the diaphyses of long bones and metapodials.

Denticle: The circular formations that form in the secondary dentine of walrus ivory.

Dentine: The dental tissue that makes up the majority of most the teeth. Ivory is synonymous with dentine.

Diaphysis: The shaft of the long bone.

Distal: The part of the skeletal element located farther from the center of the body.

Epiphysis: The end of a long bone which articulates with other skeletal elements, often composed of trabecular bone.

Enamel: Mineralized dental tissue on the exterior surface of the tooth. The enamel layer is often much thinner than the dentine layer.

Engine-Turned Lines: A name given to the Schreger Pattern due to the resemblance of the pattern to the metallic finishing technique. See "Schreger Pattern."

Haversian Canals: Part of the osteonic canal system that brings nutrients to the bone, running parallel to the length of the bone.

Keratin: A type of fibrous protein that makes up hair, fingernails, claws, hooves, horn, and baleen.

Knucklebone: A term referring to the astragalus bone, often in reference to its use in gaming.

Lamellae: Layers of growth within dentine.

Lines of Owen: The banded appearance of the concentric growth lines that make up dentine.

Medullary Cavity: The area within the diaphysis of the long bone that stores marrow. When craftspeople work long bones, the medullary cavity appears as a hollow section.

Osteon: The circular regions of concentric growth that surround haversian canals, these regions contribute to the "grainy" appearance of cortical bone.

Osteonic Canals: The Haversian and Volkmann canal systems.

Pedicle: The region where antler grows from on the cranium of the cervid.

Pulp Cavity: The region of the tooth where specialized cells form dentine. For the craftsperson carving a tooth, this portion appears as a hollow section.

Proximal: The part of the skeletal element located closer to the center of the body.

Retzius Lines: See "Schreger Pattern," not to be confused with the Striae of Retzius.

Schreger Pattern: The pattern that forms on the transverse surfaces of proboscidean ivory, often resembling cross-hatching or a checkerboard. The angles formed by this pattern can be measured as a way of differentiating different types of proboscidean taxa. It is one of the most characteristic aspects of proboscidean ivory.

Scute: A bony plate or large scale. On turtles, the term scute refers to the Keratinous scales covering the shell. Sturgeons also have rows of bony scales known as scutes.

Suture: Joints in skeletal tissue that connect different flat sections of bone. Most notably, cranial bone and the shells of turtles and tortoises possess sutures; these features can lead to confusion between two types of elements.

Tine: The forking sections of antler that terminate in conical tips.

Tortoiseshell: A name for the material made from the keratinous covering on the scutes of turtles.

Trabecular Tissue: A porous skeletal tissue that is light, and which appears spongy. Trabecular tissue can be found in the ephiphyses of long bones and throughout the center of antler.

Tusk Interstitial Zone (TIZ): An area in the center of the tooth where dentine forms, visible as a darker feature in transverse sections of teeth which are distal to the pulp cavity.

Volkmann's Canals: Part of the osteonic canal system that brings nutrients to the bone, running perpendicular to the length of the bone.

Wear Facet: A flat face that forms on teeth that are in contact with other teeth, such as on suid canines.

Whalebone: A term used to describe baleen, not to be confused with the actual bone of whales.

References

Bejenaru, L., ed. (2018), "Worked Bone and Archaeology: Proceedings of the 11th Meeting of the ICAZ Worked Bone Research Group in Iasi 2016," *Quaternary International* **472**, 1–168, www.sciencedirect.com/journal/quaternary-international/vol/472/part/PA.

Achrai, B. & Wagner, H. D. (2013), "Micro-structure and mechanical properties of the turtle carapace as a biological composite shield," *Acta Biomaterialia* 9(4), 5890–5902.

Affanni, G. (2008), "Astragalus bone in ancient near east: Ritual depositions in Iron Age I in Tell Afis," *in* J. M. Córdoba, M. Molist, M. C. Pérez, I. Rubio, & S. Martínez, eds., *Proceedings of the 5th International Congress on the Archaeology of the Ancient Near East: Madrid, April 3–8, 2006*, Madrid, Universidad Autónoma de Madrid, pp. 77–92.

Afonso, L. U., Almeida, C., & Da Silva Horta, J. (2022), "Early African ivories: The Ghana cluster," *African Arts* **55**(2), 10–19.

Arabatzis, C. (2016), "Bone industry from the prehistoric settlement Anarghiri IXa, Florina, Greece," *in* S. Vitezović, ed., *Close to the Bone. Current Studies in Bone Technologies*, Institute of Archaeology, Belgrade, pp. 9–17.

Ardelean, C. F., Arroyo-Cabrales, J., Rivera-González, I., et al. (2023), "Oldest art or symbolic expressions in North America? Pleistocene modified bones and a human remain at Sima de las Golondrinas cave, Zacatecas, Mexico," *L'Anthropologie* **127**(2), 103135.

Ashby, S. (2005), "Bone and antler combs: Towards a methodology for the understanding of trade and identity in Viking Age England and Scotland," *in* C. E. B. Heidi Luik, Alice M. Choyke, & L. Lõugas, eds., *From Hooves to Horns, from Mollusc to Mammoth: Manufacture and Use of Bone Artefacts from Prehistoric Times to the Present*, Muinasaja teadus, pp. 252–262.

Averbouh, A. & Pétillon, J.-M. (2009), "Identification of 'debitage by fracturation' on reindeer antler: Case study of the Badegoulian levels at the Cuzoul de Vers (Lot, France)," *in* B. K.-D. J. Baron, ed., *7th Meeting of the Worked Bone Research Group*, Uniwersytet Wroclawski, Instytut Archeologii, Wroclaw, pp. 41–52.

Baker, B., Jacobs, R., Mann, M., Espinoza, E., Grein, G. (2020). *CITES Identification Guide for Ivory and Ivory Substitutes* (4th Edition, Allan, C. (ed.)), World Wildlife Fund Inc., Washington DC. Commissioned by CITES Secretariat, Geneva, Switzerland.

Banerjee, A., Schuhmacher, T. X., Cardoso, J. L., et al. (2017), "Marfil de hipopótamo procedente de estratos fenicios arcaicos en Utica (Túnez)," *Sonderdruck aus Madrider Mitteilungen* **58**, 80–105.

Baron, J. & Kufel-Diakowska, B., eds. (2011), *Written in Bones: Studies on Technological and Social Contexts of Past Faunal Skeletal Remains*, Wrocław, Uniwersytet Wrocławski, Instytut Archeologii.

Barrett, J. H., Khamaiko, N., Ferrari, G., et al. (2022), "Walruses on the Dnieper: New evidence for the intercontinental trade of Greenlandic ivory in the Middle Ages," *Proceedings of the Royal Society B* **289**(1972), 1–9.

Bartels, M. H. (2005), "The Van Lidth de Jeude family and the waste from their privy: Material culture of a wealthy family in 18th-century Tiel, the Netherlands," *Northeast Historical Archaeology* **34**(1), 15–60.

Baumann, M. & Maury, S. (2013), "Ideas no longer written in antler," *Journal of Archaeological Science* **40**(1), 601–614.

Betts, M. (2007), "The Mackenzie Inuit whale bone industry: Raw material, tool manufacture, scheduling, and trade," *Arctic* **60**, 129–144.

Betts, M. W., Blair, S. E., & Black, D. W. (2012), "Perspectivism, mortuary symbolism, and human-shark relationships on the maritime peninsula," *American Antiquity* **77**(4), 621–645.

Bikić, V. & Vitezović, S. (2016), "Bone working and the army: An early eighteenth-century button workshop at the Belgrade fortress," *in* S. Vitezović, ed., *Close to the Bone. Current Studies in Bone Technologies*, Institute of Archaeology, Belgrade, pp. 57–65.

Bläuer, A., Hukantaival, S., Saarinen, R., Hirvilammi, M., & Ratilainen, T. (2019), "Early medieval/viking age exchange networks: Cattle phalanx gaming pieces from Turku, Finland," *Lund Archaeological Review*, pp. 5–25.

Boardman, J. (1967), *Excavations in Chios, 1952–1955: Greek Emporio*, number 6 *in* "*BSA* Suppl," British School of Archaeology at Athens.

Bordes, F. (1961), *Typologie du Paléolithique Ancien et Moyen*, l'Université de Bordeaux.

Breuil, H. (1907), "La question Aurignacienne: étude critique de stratigraphie comparée," *Revue Préhistorique* **2**, 1–47.

Campana, D. V. (1989), *Natufian and Protoneolithic Bone Tools: The Manufacture and Use of Bone Implements in the Zagros and the Levant*, Vol. 494, British Archaeological Reports.

Carè, B., ed. (Forthcoming), *Astragalomania: New Perspectives in the Study of Knucklebones in the Ancient World*, De Gruyter.

Casson, L. (1989), *The Periplus Maris Erythraei: Text with Introduction, Translation, and Commentary*, Princeton University Press.

Chauvet, G. (1910), *Os ivoires et bois de renne ouvrés de la Charente. Hypothèses paléthnographiques*, Bulletins et Mémoires de la Société d'Anthropologie de Paris (8° Série), E. Constantin, Angoulême.

Chechushkov, I. V., Epimakhov, A. V., & Bersenev, A. G. (2018), "Early horse bridle with cheekpieces as a marker of social change: An experimental and statistical study," *Journal of Archaeological Science* 97, 125–136.

Childe, V., Paterson, J. & Bryce, T. (1929), "Provisional report on the excavations at Skara Brae, and on finds from the 1927 and 1928 campaigns," *Proceedings of the Society of Antiquaries of Scotland* 63, 225–280.

Choyke, A. M. & Bartosiewicz, L., eds. (2001), *Crafting Bone: Skeletal Technologies through Time and Space – Proceedings of the 2nd Meeting of the (ICAZ) Worked Bone Research Group*, number 937, Oxford, British Archaeological Reports.

Choyke, A. M., Vretemark, M., & Sten, S. (2004), "Levels of social identity expressed in the refuse and worked bone from Middle Bronze Age Százhalombatta-Földvár, Vatya culture, Hungary," *in Behaviour Behind Bones: The Zooarchaeology of Ritual, Religion, Status and Identity* S. J. O'Day, W. V. Neer, A. Ervynck, eds., Vol. 1, Oxford, Oxbow Books, pp. 177–189.

Choyke, A. M. & Schibler, J. (2007), "Prehistoric bone tools and the archaeozoological perspective: Research in Central Europe," *in* C. G. St-Pierre & R. B. Walker, eds., *Bones as Tools: Current Methods and Interpretations in Worked Bone Studies*, British Archaeological Reports, Oxford, BAR Publishing, pp. 51–65.

Choyke, A. M. & Tóth, Z. (2013), "Practice makes perfect: Quartered metapodial awls in the Late Neolithic of Hungary," *in* A. Anders & G. Kulcsár, eds., *Moments in Time: Papers Presented to Pál Raczky on His 60th Birthday*, pp. 337–352.

Clark, J. G. D. & Thompson, M. W. (1954), "The groove and splinter technique of working antler in Upper Palaeolithic and Mesolithic Europe," *Proceedings of the Prehistoric Society* 19(2), 148–160.

Conneller, C. (2012), *An Archaeology of Materials: Substantial Transformations in Early Prehistoric Europe*, New York, Routledge.

Cristiani, E., Živaljević, I., & Borić, D. (2014), "Residue analysis and ornament suspension techniques in prehistory: Cyprinid pharyngeal teeth beads from Late Mesolithic burials at Vlasac (Serbia)," *Journal of Archaeological Science* 46, 292–310.

Davies, W. (2009), "The Abbé Henri Breuil (1877–1961)," *in* R. Hosfield, F. Wenban-Smith, & M. Pope, eds., *Great Prehistorians: 150 Years of Palaeolithic Research, 1859–2009*, Vol. 30 of *Lithics: The Journal of the Lithic Studies Society*, Lithic Studies Society, London, pp. 127–141.

Davis, D. D., Kidder, T. R., & Barondess, D. A. (1983), "Reduction analysis of simple bone industries: An example from the Louisiana Coastal Zone," *Archaeology of Eastern North America* **11**, 98–108.

de Mortillet, G. (1873), *Classification des diverses périodes de l'âge de la pierre*, P. Weissenbruch.

Dominy, N. J., Mills, S. T., Yakacki, C. M., Roscoe, P. B., & Carpenter, R. D. (2018), "New Guinea bone daggers were engineered to preserve social prestige," *Royal Society Open Science* **5**(4), 1–12.

Edwards, H., Hunt, D., & Sibley, M. (1998a), "FT-Raman spectroscopic study of keratotic materials: horn, hoof and tortoiseshell," *Spectrochimica Acta Part A: Molecular and Biomolecular Spectroscopy* **54**(5), 745–757.

Edwards, H. G. M., Farwell, D. W., Holder, J. M., & Lawson, E. E. (1998b), "Fourier Transform-Raman spectroscopy of ivory: A non-destructive diagnostic technique," *Studies in Conservation* **43**(1), 9–16.

Espinoza, E. O., Baker, B. W., & Berry, C. A. (2007), "The analysis of sea turtle and bovid keratin artefacts using drift spectroscopy and discriminant analysis," *Archaeometry* **49**(4), 685–698.

Espinoza, E. O. & Mann, M.-J. (1992), *Identification Guide for Ivory and Ivory Substitutes*, Baltimore, MD, World Wildlife Fund and Conservation Foundation.

Espinoza, E. O. & Mann, M.-J. (1993), "The history and significance of the schreger pattern in proboscidean ivory characterization," *Journal of the American Institute for Conservation* **32**(3), 241–248.

Evans, S. J. (2021), Finding Moby: Novel approaches to identifying human-cetacean relationships in Atlantic Scotland from c. 2500 BC to c. AD 1400, PhD thesis, Cardiff University.

Fernández-Jalvo, Y. & Andrews, P. (2016), *Atlas of Taphonomic Identifications: 1001+ Images of Fossil and Recent Mammal Bone Modification*, Dordrecht Springer.

Fisher, J. W. (1995), "Bone surface modifications in zooarchaeology," *Journal of Archaeological Method and Theory* **2**(1), 7–68.

Frazier, J. (2002), "Prehistoric and ancient historic interactions between humans and marine turtles," *in* P. L. Lutz, J. A. Musick & J. Wyneken, eds., *The Biology of Sea Turtles*, Vol. II, Boca Raton, FL, CRC press, 1–38.

Frazier, J. & Ishihara-Brito, R. (2012), "The occurrence of tortoiseshell on a pre-Hispanic Maya mosaic mask," *Antiquity* **86**(333), 825–837.

Frenez, D. (2018), "Manufacturing and trade of Asian elephant ivory in Bronze Age Middle Asia. Evidence from Gonur Depe (Margiana, Turkmenistan)," *Archaeological Research in Asia* **15**, 13–33.

Gillreath-Brown, A. (2019), "Creation to rhythm: An ethnographic and archaeological survey of turtle shell rattles and spirituality in the united states," *Journal of Ethnobiology* **39**(3), 425–444.

Gilmour, G. H. (1997), "The nature and function of astragalus bones from archaeological contexts in the Levant and eastern Mediterranean," *Oxford Journal of Archaeology* **16**(2), 167–175.

Girya, E. Y. & Khlopachev, G. A. (2019), "Experimental data on the splitting and knapping of mammoth tusks and reindeer antlers," *in* M. Christensen & N. Goutas, eds., *À coup d'éclats!: la fracturation des matières osseuses en préhistoire : discussion autour d'une modalité d'exploitation en apparence simple et pourtant mal connue*, Société préhistorique française, Paris, pp. 325–340.

González, F. M., ed. (2019), *Cuadernos de Prehistoria y Arqueología de la Universidad de Granada*, Vol. 29.

Goss, R. J. (1983), *Deer Antlers. Regeneration, Function and Evolution*, Academic Press, New York.

Hahn, J. (1972), "Aurignacian signs, pendants and art objects in Central and Eastern Europe," *World Archaeology* **3**(3), 252–266.

Haines, H. R., Willink, P. W., & Maxwell, D. (2008), "Stingray spine use and Maya bloodletting rituals: A cautionary tale," *Latin American Antiquity* **19**(1), 83–98.

Hamilton, S. & Nicholson, B. (2007), "The middleman fur trade and slot knives: Selective integration of European technology at the Mortiach Twin Fawns site (DiMe-23)," *Canadian Journal of Archaeology / Journal Canadien d'Archéologie* **31**(3), 137–162.

Hanausek, T. F. (1907), *The Microscopy of Technical Products*, New York, John Wiley & Sons.

Heckel, C. E. & Wolf, S. (2014), "Ivory debitage by fracture in the Aurignacian: experimental and archaeological examples," *Journal of Archaeological Science* **42**, 1–14.

Henshilwood, C. S., D'errico, F., Marean, C. W., Milo, R. G., & Yates, R. (2001), "An early bone tool industry from the middle stone age at Blombos Cave, South Africa: Implications for the origins of modern human behaviour, symbolism and language," *Journal of Human Evolution* **41**(6), 631–678.

Herrmann, G. (2017), *Ancient Ivory*, London, Thames & Hudson.

Hillson, S. (2005), *Teeth*, Cambridge Manuals in Archaeology, Cambridge, Cambridge University Press.

Hofman, J. L. (1980), "Scapula skin-dressing and fiber-processing tools," *Plains Anthropologist* **25**(88), 135–142.

Huelsbeck, D. R. (1988), "Whaling in the precontact economy of the central northwest coast," *Arctic Anthropology* **25**(1), 1–15.

Hull, J. R. (2018), "Bringing culture back into focus: Osseous implements from southern Vietnam," *Journal of Archaeological Science: Reports* **20**, 937–951.

Isaakidou, V. (2017), "Meaningful materials? bone artefacts and symbolism in the Early Bronze Age Aegean," *Oxford Journal of Archaeology* **36**(1), 43–59.

James, E. C. & Thompson, J. C. (2015), "On bad terms: Problems and solutions within zooarchaeological bone surface modification studies," *Environmental Archaeology* **20**(1), 89–103.

Jonuks, T. & Rannamäe, E. (2018), "Animals and worldviews: A diachronic approach to tooth and bone pendants from the Mesolithic to the Medieval Period in Estonia," *in* A. Livarda, R. Madgwick & S. R. Mora, eds., *The Bioarchaeology of Ritual and Religion*, Oxford, Oxbow Books pp. 162–178.

Jowsey, J. (1966), "Studies of haversian systems in man and some animals," *Journal of Anatomy* **100**, 857–864.

Kendig, W. E., Smith, K. N., Vellanoweth, R. L., et al. (2010), "The use of replicative studies in understanding the function of expedient tools: The sandstone saws of San Nicolas Island, California," *Journal of California and Great Basin Anthropology* **30**(2), 193–210.

Klippel, W. E. & Price, B. E. (2007), "Bone disc manufacturing debris from Newfoundland to Antigua during the Historic Period," *in* C. G. St-Pierre & R. B. Walker, eds., *Bones as Tools: Current Methods and Interpretations in Worked Bone Studies*, British Archaeological Reports, Oxford, BAR Publishing, pp. 133–142.

Koitabashi, M. (2013), "An incised scapula from Kaman–Kalehöyük – A a musical scraper?," *Anatolian Archaeological Studies* **18**, 43–48.

Kokkoliou, A. (2020), "A Classical Athenian grave (no 48, 470–50 bc) and its content from the area between the so-called 'Ēriai' Gate and the Dipylon: The archaeological context," *Greek and Roman Musical Studies* **8**(2), 279–309.

Krzyszkowska, O. (1988), "Ivory in the Aegean Bronze Age: Elephant tusk or hippopotamus ivory?" *The Annual of the British School at Athens* **83**, 209–234.

Krzyszkowska, O. (1990), *Ivory and Related Materials: An Illustrated Guide*, number 59 *in* "*BICS* Suppl.", Institute of Classical Studies.

Lang, F., ed. (2013), *The Sound of Bones. Proceedings of the 8th Meeting of the ICAZ Worked Bone Research Group in Salzburg 2011*, number 5 *in* "Archaeo plus," Eigenverl. Univ. Salzburg, Interfakultärer Fachbereich Gerichtsmedizin.

Langley, M. C., O'Connor, S., & Aplin, K. (2016), "A 46,000-year-old kangaroo bone implement from Carpenter's Gap 1 (Kimberley, Northwest Australia)," *Quaternary Science Reviews* **154**, 199–213.

Lapatin, K. D. (2001), *Chryselephantine Statuary in the Ancient Mediterranean World*, Oxford Monographs on Classical Archaeology, Oxford, Oxford University Press.

Lárusdóttir, B., Roberts, H. M., & þorgeirsdóttir, S. (2012), Siglunes: Archaeological investigations in 2011, Technical report.

Lauffenburger, J. A. (1993), "Baleen in museum collections: Its sources, uses, and identification," *Journal of the American Institute for Conservation* **32**(3), 213–230.

Leach, B. F., Davidson, J., McCallum, G., et al. (1979), 'The identification of dugong ivory reel artefacts from strontium content and microstructure', *New Zealand Journal of Archaeology* **1**, 115–121.

Leder, D., Hermann, R., Hüls, M., et al. (2021), "A 51,000-year-old engraved bone reveals neanderthals' capacity for symbolic behaviour," *Nature Ecology & Evolution* **5**(9), 1273–1282.

Lee, P. B. & Nijman, V. (2015), "Trade in dugong parts in southern Bali," *Journal of the Marine Biological Association of the United Kingdom* **95**(8), 1717–1721.

Legrand-Pineau, A., Sidéra, I., Buc, N., David, E. & Scheinsohn, V., eds. (2010), *Ancient and Modern Bone Artefacts from America to Russia: Cultural, Technological and Functional Signature*, Vol. 2136 of *British Archaeological Reports International Series*, Oxford Archaeopress.

LeMoine, G. M. & Darwent, C. M. (1998), "The walrus and the carpenter: Late Dorset ivory working in the high arctic," *Journal of Archaeological Science* **25**(1), 73–83.

Lisowski, M. (2014), "Hides and horn sheaths: A case study of processed skulls and horn cores from the Early-Middle Neolithic site of Kopydłowo 6, Poland," *Assemblage PZAF*, pp. 32–41.

Locke, M. (2008), "Structure of ivory," *Journal of Morphology* **269**(4), 423–450.

Luciañez-Triviño, M., García Sanjuán, L., & Schuhmacher, T. (2022), "Crafting idiosyncrasies: Early social complexity, ivory and identity-making in Copper Age Iberia," *Cambridge Archaeological Journal* **32**(1), 23–60.

Luik, H. (2012), "Bone artefacts from the Keava hill fort and Linnaaluste settlement sites," *Estonian Journal of Archaeology* **16**(1S) 92–105.

Luik, H., Choyke, A. M., Batey, C. E., & Lõugas, L., eds. (2005), *From Hooves to Horns, from Mollusc to Mammoth: Manufacture and Use of Bone Artefacts from Prehistoric Times to the Present*, Tallinn Muinasaja teadus.

Lyman, R. L. (1994), *Vertebrate Taphonomy*, Cambridge Manuals in Archaeology, Cambridge Cambridge University Press.

Ma, X. & Hou, Y., eds. (2014), *Proceedings of the 9th Meeting of the (ICAZ) Worked Bone Research Group, Zhengzhou, China, 2013*, number 2 *in* "Zooarchaeology," Culture Relics Press.

MacGregor, A. (1985), *Bone, Antler, Ivory and Horn*, Totowa NJ Barnes & Noble Books.

Majkić, A., d'Errico, F., Milošević, S., Mihailović, D., & Dimitrijević, V. (2018), "Sequential incisions on a cave bear bone from the Middle Paleolithic of Pešturina Cave, Serbia," *Journal of Archaeological Method and Theory* **25**, 69–116.

Makariou, S. (2010), "The al-Mughīra Pyxis and Spanish Umayyad Ivories: Aims and tools of power," *in* A. Borrut and P. M. Cobb, eds., *Umayyad legacies: medieval memories from Syria to Spain*, number 80 *in Islamic history and civilization*, Brill, Leiden, pp. 313–335.

Mannermaa, K., Rainio, R., Girya, E. Y., & Gerasimov, D. V. (2020), "Let's groove: Attachment techniques of Eurasian elk (*Alces alces*) tooth pendants at the Late Mesolithic cemetery Yuzhniy Oleniy Ostrov (Lake Onega, Russia)," *Archaeological and Anthropological Sciences* **13**(1) 1–22, https://link.springer.com/article/10.1007/s12520-020-01237-5.

McGrath, K., Rowsell, K., Gates St-Pierre, C., et al. (2019), "Identifying archaeological bone via non-destructive ZooMS and the materiality of symbolic expression: Examples from Iroquoian bone points," *Scientific Reports* **9**(1), 11027.

McNiven, I. J. (2010), "Navigating the human-animal divide: Marine mammal hunters and rituals of sensory allurement," *World Archaeology* **42**(2), 215–230.

Medina, M., López, L., & Buc, N. (2018), "Bone tool and tuber processing: A multi-proxy approach at Boyo Paso 2, Argentina," *Antiquity* **92**(364), 1040–1055.

Mehendale, S. (2001), "The Begram ivory and bone carvings: Some observations on provenance and chronology," *Topoi: Orient-Occident* **11**(1), 485–514.

Miles, A. E. W. & White, J. W. (1960), "Ivory," *Proceedings of the Royal Society of Medicine* **53**(9), 775–780.

Moffat, R., Spriggs, J., & O'Connor, S. (2008), "The use of baleen for arms, armour and heraldic crests in medieval Britain," *The Antiquaries Journal* **88**, 207–215.

Mouël, J.-F. L. & Mouël, M. L. (2002), "Aspects of Early Thule culture as seen in the architecture of a site on Victoria Island, Amundsen Gulf area," *Arctic* **55**(2), 167–189.

Nganvongpanit, K., Buddhachat, K., Kaewmong, P., Cherdsukjai, P., & Kittiwatanawong, K. (2017), "What the skull and scapular morphology of the dugong (*Dugong dugon*) can tell us: Sex, habitat and body length?" *Scientific Reports* **7**(1), 1964.

Nishida, A. (2016), "Old Tibetan scapulimancy," *Revue d'Etudes Tibétaines* **37**, 262–277.

O'Connor, S. (1987), "The identification of osseous and keratinaceous materials at York," *in* K. Starling & D. Watkinson, eds., *Archaeological Bone, Antler and Ivory: The Proceedings of a Conference Held by UKIC Archaeology Section, December 1984 / United Kingdom Institute for Conservation*, London, United Kingdom Institute for Conservation, pp. 9–21.

O'Connor, S. (2016), "The COWISHT project: Enhancing the identification of artefact raw materials," *Cuadernos del Instituto Nacional de Antropologia y Pensamiento Latinoamericano–Series Especiales* **3**(2), 4–22.

O'Connor, S. & O'Connor, T. (2017), "Reconsideration of the 'Mesolithic harpoon' from Westward Ho! Devon," *in* P. Rowley-Conwy, D. Serjeantson, & P. Halstead, eds., *Economic Zooarchaeology: Studies in Hunting, Herding and Early Agriculture*, Oxford, Oxbow Books.

O'Connor, S., Solazzo, C., & Collins, M. (2015), "Advances in identifying archaeological traces of horn and other keratinous hard tissues," *Studies in Conservation* **60**(6), 393–417.

Okaluk, T. R. & Greenfield, H. J. (2022), "Macroscopic chop mark identification on archaeological bone: An experimental study of chipped stone, ground stone, copper, and bronze axe heads on bone," *Quaternary* **5**(1), 15.

Osipowicz, G. (2007), "Bone and antler: Softening techniques in prehistory of the north eastern part of the Polish Lowlands in the light of experimental archaeology and micro trace analysis," *EXARC* **4**, 1–22.

Owen, R. (1856), "The ivory and teeth of commerce," *Journal of the Society of Arts* **5**(213), 65–73.

Paillet, P. (1999), "Le bison dans les arts magdaléniens du Périgord," *Gallia préhistoire: Suppléments* (33), 1–475.

Papadopoulos, J. K. & Ruscillo, D. (2002), "A *Ketos* in early Athens: An archaeology of whales and sea monsters in the Greek world," *American Journal of Archaeology* **106**(2), 187–227.

Pawłowska, K. & Barański, M. Z. (2020), "Conceptualization of the Neolithic world in incised equid phalanges: Anthropomorphic figurine from

Çatalhöyük (GDN area)," *Archaeological and Anthropological Sciences* **12**(1), 18.

Pedersen, M. C. (2004), *Gem and Ornamental Materials of Organic Origin*, Oxford, Elsevier Butterworth-Heinemann.

Penniman, T. (1952), *Pictures of Ivory and Other Animal Teeth Bone and Antler*, number 5 *in* "Occasional Papers on Technology," Oxford University Press.

Peres, T. M. & Altman, H. (2018), "The magic of improbable appendages: Deer antler objects in the archaeological record of the American South," *Journal of Archaeological Science: Reports* **20**, 888–895.

Pétillon, J.-M. (2013), "Circulation of whale-bone artifacts in the northern Pyrenees during the late Upper Paleolithic," *Journal of Human Evolution* **65**(5), 525–543.

Pétillon, J.-M. & Ducasse, S. (2012), "From flakes to grooves: A technical shift in antlerworking during the last glacial maximum in southwest France," *Journal of Human Evolution* **62**(4), 435–465.

Raubenheimer, E. J. (1999), "Morphological aspects and composition of African elephant (*Loxodonta africana*) ivory," *Journal of Morphology* **42**(2), 57–64.

Reese, D. S. (2005), "Whale bones and shell purple-dye at Motya (Western Sicily, Italy)," *Oxford Journal of Archaeology* **24**(2), 107–114.

Reitz, E. J. & Wing, E. S. (1999), *Zooarchaeology*, 2 edn, Cambridge, Cambridge University Press.

Retzius, A. A. (1837), "Bemerkungen über den innern Bau der Zähne, mit besonderer Rücksicht auf den im Zahnknochen vorkommenden Röhrenbau," in *Archiv für Anatomie, Physiologie und Wissenschaftliche Medicin*, pp. 486–566, https://www.biodiversitylibrary.org/item/49864#page/7/mode/1up.

Richter, K. K., Codlin, M. C., Seabrook, M. & Warinner, C. (2022), "A primer for ZooMS applications in archaeology," *Proceedings of the National Academy of Sciences* **119**(20), 1–10.

Riddler, I., ed. (2003), *Materials of Manufacture: The Choice of Materials in the Working of Bone and Antler in Northern and Ventral Europe during the First Millennium AD*, Vol. 1193 of *British Archaeological Reports International Series*, Oxford, Archaeopress.

Rijkelijkhuizen, M. (2009), "Whales, walruses, and elephants: Artisans in ivory, baleen, and other skeletal materials in seventeenth- and eighteenth-century Amsterdam," *International Journal of Historical Archaeology* **13**(4), 409–429.

Russell, N. (2005), "Çatalhöyük worked bone," *in* I. Hodder, ed., *Changing Materialities at Çatalhöyük: Reports from the 1995–99 Seasons*, Vol. 39, London, British Institute at Ankara, pp. 339–368.

Sayers, W. (1992), "Scapulimancy in the medieval Baltic," *Journal of Baltic Studies* **23**(1), 57–62.

Schibler, J. (1981), *Die neolithischen Ufersiedlungen von Twann. Band 17: Typologische Untersuchungen der cortaillodzeitlichen Knochenartefakte*, Staatlicher Lehrmittelverlag Bern.

Schibler, J. (2012), "Bone and antler artefacts in wetland sites," *in* F. Menotti & A. O'Sullivan, eds., *The Oxford Handbook of Wetland Archaeology*, Oxford, Oxford University Press, pp. 340–355.

Schreger, B. N. G. (1800), "Beitrag zur Geschichte der Zähne," *Beiträge für die Zergliederungskunst* **1**, 1–7.

Sellet, F. (1993), "*Chaîne Opératoire*: The concept and its applications," *Lithic Technology* **18**(1/2), 106–112.

Semenov, S. (1964), *Prehistoric Technology: An Experimental Study of the Oldest Tools and Artefacts from Traces of Manufacture and Wear*, Totowa, NJ Barnes and Noble Books.

Shen, C. (2002), *Anyang and Sanxingdui: Unveiling the Mysteries of Ancient Chinese Civilizations*, Royal Ontario Museum, Toronto.

Shott, M. J. (2003), "Chaîne Opératoire and reduction sequence," *Lithic Technology* **28**(2), 95–105.

Sinding, M.-H. S., Gilbert, M. T. P., Grønnow, B., et al. (2012), "Minimally destructive DNA extraction from archaeological artefacts made from whale baleen," *Journal of Archaeological Science* **39**(12), 3750–3753.

Smith, G. D. & Clark, R. J. (2004), "Raman microscopy in archaeological science," *Journal of Archaeological Science* **31**(8), 1137–1160.

Solazzo, C., Fitzhugh, W., Kaplan, S., Potter, C. & Dyer, J. M. (2017), "Molecular markers in keratins from mysticeti whales for species identification of baleen in museum and archaeological collections," *PLoS One* **12**(8), 1–24.

St-Pierre, C. G., Needs-Howarth, S., & Boisvert, M. (2021), "Indicators for interactions from legacy worked and unworked faunal assemblages from the Quackenbush site, a Late Woodland site in the Kawartha Lakes region, Ontario," *Canadian Journal of Archaeology* **45**(2), 230–258.

St-Pierre, C. G. & Walker, R. B., eds. (2007), *Bones as Tools: Current Methods and Interpretations in Worked Bone Studies*, number 1622, British Archaeological Reports, Oxford, Archaeopress.

Stern, W. (2007), *Ivory, Bone, and Related Wood Finds*, Brill, Leiden.

Tanner, A. (1978), Divinations and decisions: multiple explanations for algonkian scapulimancy, *in* E. Schwimmer, ed., The Yearbook of Symbolic Anthropology I, Montreal, McGill-Queen's University Press, pp. 89–101.

Thorson, R. M. & Guthrie, R. D. (1984), "River ice as a taphonomic agent: An alternative hypothesis for bone 'artifacts'," *Quaternary Research* **22**(2), 172–188.

Trapani, J. & Fisher, D. C. (2003), "Discriminating proboscidean taxa using features of the schreger pattern in tusk dentin," *Journal of Archaeological Science* **30**(4), 429–438.

Uerpmann, M., de Beauclair, R., Händel, M., et al. (2012), "The Neolithic site FAY-NE15 in the central region of the Emirate of Sharjah (UAE)," *Proceedings of the Seminar for Arabian Studies* **42**, 385–400.

van den Hurk, Y., Riddler, I., McGrath, K., & Speller, C. (2023), "Active whaling, opportunistic scavenging or long-distance trading: Zooarchaeological, palaeoproteomic, and historical analyses on whale exploitation and bone working in Anglo-Saxon Hamwic," *Medieval Archaeology* **67**(1), 137–158.

van Leeuwenhoek, A. (1678), "Microscopical observations of the structure of teeth and other bones: Made and communicated, in a letter by Mr. Anthony Leeuwenhoeck," *Philosophical Transactions of the Royal Society of London* **12**(140), 1002–1003.

Virág, A. (2012), "Histogenesis of the unique morphology of proboscidean ivory," *Journal of Morphology* **273**(12), 1406–1423.

Vitezović, S., ed. (2016), *Close to the Bone: Current Studies in Bone Technologies*, Institute of Archaeology, Belgrade.

Wake, T. (2001), "Bone tool technology on Santa Cruz Island and implications for exchange," *in* J. E. Arnold, ed., *The Origins of a Pacific Coast Chiefdom: The Chumash of the Channel Islands*, University of Utah Press, pp. 183–198.

Walker, K. J. (1992), "Bone artifacts from Josslyn Island, Buck Key Shell Midden, and Cash Mound: A preliminary assessment for the Caloosahatchee Area," *in* W. H. Marquardt & C. Payne, eds., *Culture and Environment in the Domain of the Calusa*, number 1 *in Monograph / Institute of Archaeology and Paleoenvironmental Studies, University of Florida*, Institute of Archaeology and Paleoenvironmental Studies, Gainesville, University of Florida, pp. 230–246.

Wang, B., Sullivan, T. N., Pissarenko, A., et al. (2019), "Lessons from the ocean: Whale baleen fracture resistance," *Advanced Materials* **31**(3), 1804574.

Wang, H., Campbell, R., Fang, H., Hou, Y., & Li, Z. (2022), "Small-scale bone working in a complex economy: The Daxinzhuang worked bone assemblage," *Journal of Anthropological Archaeology* **66**, 101411.

Wild, M., Thurber, B. A., Rhodes, S., & Gates St-Pierre, C., eds. (2021), *Bones at a Crossroads: Integrating Worked Bone Research with Archaeometry and Social Zooarchaeology*, Sidestone Press.

Xie, L., Lu, X., Sun, G., & Huang, W. (2017), "Functionality and morphology: Identifying Si agricultural tools from among Hemudu scapular implements in Eastern China," *Journal of Archaeological Method and Theory* **24**(2), 377–423.

Zhilin, M. G. (1998), "Technology of the manufacture of Mesolithic bone arrowheads on the Upper Volga," *European Journal of Archaeology* **1**(2), 149–176.

Zukerman, A., Lev-Tov, J., Kolska-Horwitz, L., & Maeir, A. M. (2007), "A bone of contention? Iron Age IIA notched scapulae from Tell eş-Sâfî/Gath, Israel," *Bulletin of the American Schools of Oriental Research* **347**, 57–81.

Acknowledgments

This Element was the result of an invitation by Hans Barnard, Willeke Wendrich, and Beatrice Rehl, and I thank them for the opportunity and support throughout the publishing process. My interest in this topic began at the Cotsen Institute of Archaeology, where I was surrounded by generous colleagues and mentors. John Papadopoulos and Sarah Morris have been constant supporters of my work, and I remain grateful to them for allowing me to study the Methone assemblage. Thank you also to the Pieria Ephoria and my other collaborators from Methone, especially Jeff Vanderpool, whose photography was a major benefit to this Element. I began writing this Element at the Institute of the Study of the Ancient World (ISAW) at New York University, which provided crucial financial and institutional support. The resources of ISAW allowed me to visit the Bromage Lab; Timothy Bromage and his collaborators were immensely generous with their time, and I thank them for creating splendid images of dental tissue. I completed this Element at the American School of Classical Studies at Athens, which provided an amazing environment for research and collaboration. Thank you to my parents for their support; my mother's willingness to read drafts made this possible! Thank you to Jordan Berson and the rest of the staff of the New Bedford Whaling Museum for allowing me to study the collection and see a narwhal tusk up close! I owe a debt of thanks to Alice Choyke, whose work inspired me long before I wrote this Element. Finally, I am so grateful for the support of Leah Olson, an amazing artist who I rely on for so much more than her drawings!

Cambridge Elements ≡

Current Archaeological Tools and Techniques

Hans Barnard
Cotsen Institute of Archaeology

Hans Barnard was associate adjunct professor in the Department of Near Eastern Languages and Cultures as well as associate researcher at the Cotsen Institute of Archaeology, both at the University of California, Los Angeles. He currently works at the Roman site of Industria in northern Italy and previously participated in archaeological projects in Armenia, Chile, Egypt, Ethiopia, Italy, Iceland, Panama, Peru, Sudan, Syria, Tunisia, and Yemen. This is reflected in the seven books and more than 100 articles and chapters to which he contributed.

Willeke Wendrich
Polytechnic University of Turin

Willeke Wendrich is Professor of Cultural Heritage and Digital Humanities at the Politecnico di Torino (Turin, Italy). Until 2023 she was Professor of Egyptian Archaeology and Digital Humanities at the University of California, Los Angeles, and the first holder of the Joan Silsbee Chair in African Cultural Archaeology. Between 2015 and 2023 she was Director of the Cotsen Institute of Archaeology, with which she remains affiliated. She managed archaeological projects in Egypt, Ethiopia, Italy, and Yemen, and is on the board of the International Association of Egyptologists, Museo Egizio (Turin, Italy), the Institute for Field Research, and the online UCLA Encyclopedia of Egyptology.

About the Series

Cambridge University Press and the Cotsen Institute of Archaeology at UCLA collaborate on this series of Elements, which aims to facilitate deployment of specific techniques by archaeologists in the field and in the laboratory. It provides readers with a basic understanding of selected techniques, followed by clear instructions how to implement them, or how to collect samples to be analyzed by a third party, and how to approach interpretation of the results.

COTSEN INSTITUTE OF
ARCHAEOLOGY AT UCLA

Cambridge Elements ☰

Current Archaeological Tools and Techniques

Elements in the Series

A full series listing is available at: www.cambridge.org/EATT